PLUM ISLAND 2018
TWO STEPS FORWARD, THREE STEPS BACK

TABLE OF CONTENTS

Acknowledgements

I have mentioned most of the people who helped me gather material for this book in the text. However, I would like to especially thank several people who went way beyond the call of duty.

They include Becky Coburn who designed the cover and stewarded the manuscript through the entire publication process.

They include my friend and inestimable editor Richard Lodge at the Newburyport Daily, where many of these chapters were first published.

They also include the excellent photographers, Ethan Cohen and Sandy Tilton. Sandy uses her keen eye to observe the beauty of coastal processes while Ethan uses his drone to give us the big picture. Andy Griffith and Plum Island Outdoors have given us the opportunity to do much of this photography.

I would also like to thank the good people at the Quebec Labrador Foundation, The Sounds Conservancy, the Institution for Savings, and Plum Island Outdoors for providing grants to help fund the research for this book.

And most of all I'd like to thank Kristina and Chappell for putting up with my spending long stormy nights up to my keister in cold water and long steamy days sitting on my keister typing in our attic.

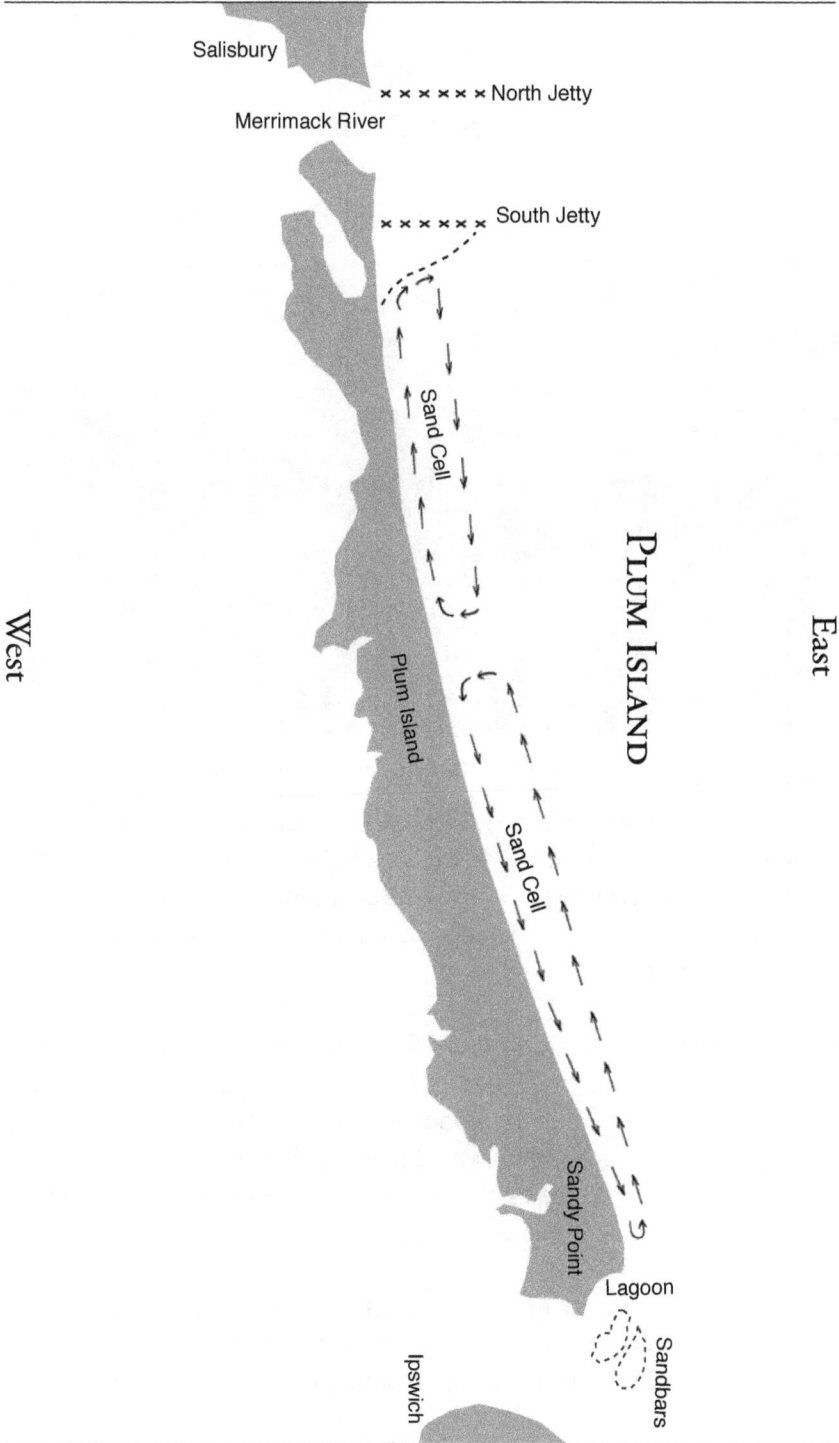

Salisbury

× × × × × North Jetty

Merrimack River

× × × × × South Jetty

Sand Cell

West

East

PLUM ISLAND

Plum Island

Sand Cell

Sandy Point

Lagoon

Sandbars

Ipswich

CHAPTER I
Sandy Point
August 1, 2017

Sandy Point. photo by UAVLook.

On August 1, I drove to Sandy Point on Plum Island's south end. It was a long beautiful ride from my home in Ipswich, Massachusetts. On my right, the sun shown down on the rivers, creeks and marshes of Plum Island Sound and on my left it filtered through row upon row of buttery green corn fields.

I took a right as I entered Plum Island and soon I was on the long dusty road that leads to the end of the island. Every once in a while I would see a cloud of dust approaching, then it would resolve into two headlights and a Land Rover would rush by. It reminded me of driving over the lava-covered roads of Iceland where people were so happy to see another car they would wave madly at each other as they drove by.

I finally reached Sandy Point and gazed across the water at my own house. It had taken me an hour to drive here from Ipswich. If I had just paddled across Plum Island Sound it would have taken me ten minutes.

But I wouldn't have had my camera, so I resolved to buy a dry bag for my future expeditions.

I had come out here on August 1 because that is what I consider to be the start of the erosion season. It is exactly halfway through the hurricane season but it is in the latter part of the season, August, September and October, when the most powerful storms form off Africa, then cross the Atlantic and work their way up the East Coast toward New England.

Just a few days before, the north end of the island had been pummeled by long period waves. These had been created by an offshore storm that traveled unnoticed until it reached the shallow waters of a sandbar in the mouth of the Merrimack River. This had caused the long period waves, which had only been a few feet high out at sea to build to about six feet and break right against the dunes.

The waves had already removed about 5 feet off the face of the dunes and the houses on Northern Reservation Terrace couldn't afford losing any more of the dunes that protected them. Last winter they lost 75 feet because the state had built a sacrificial dune, the year before they had lost 150 feet and now many of the houses were less than a hundred feet from the edge.

This was because the Army Corps of Engineers had cut off the flow of sand to the area by repairing the Merrimack River's south jetty. It was clear that the 2018 erosion season was going to be crucial to the future of the north end of the island.

But you never hear about erosion on the south end of the island. This is because it has no structures and is far from the groins, jetties and seawalls that increase erosion on other parts of the island. However, just as much erosion occurs out here. I could see the eroding cliff and wide boulder field of Emerson's rocks exposed at low tide. This is where the ocean has been steadily scarping the cliffs of one of the major drumlins underpinning the island.

These drumlins were abandoned on the landscape as the glaciers retreated, and during the past 4,000 years Plum Island has been slowly migrated as the seas have rising to its present location perched on several of these gravel and boulder filled drumlins.

But this uninhabited end of the island is also growing. A grandmother and her two grandchildren were happily playing in a long thin tide pool in the sand. The family had set up a gazebo on a sandbar on the opposite side of the tide pool.

This sandbar is what geologists call a recurving spit. It is composed of sand that has flowed south from the center of the island. As these spits grow they encircle bodies of water creating these long thin tide pools. Sometimes they can create a cove deep enough for boats to anchor, but eventually the spit will close off the cove and it can even fill with rainwater to become a freshwater pond. In this manner the south end of the island grows several hundred feet a year creating tide pools and sometimes freshwater ponds and swamps in its wake.

Other sandbars have been swept offshore to form part of the ebb tide delta that bulges into the ocean beyond the mouth of Plum Island Sound. When you have a Northeaster, sand can skirt around the ebb tide delta and end up on the other side of the Sound. This forms another sandbar that parallels Crane Beach. But the sandbar doesn't stay still. Waves constantly cause it to roll over itself so that it migrates toward the shore.

This creates a fascinating recreational area but a huge headache for the Trustees of Reservations who manage Crane Beach. As the sandbar draws closer to the shore it becomes swimmable from the beach and a great place to land boats. During the summer you might have as many as 50 boats on the sandbar.

Several years ago a local radio station set up shop on the island along with hundreds of barefoot revelers who had swum across the current filled isthmus. I remember watching all summer as the gap between the beach and the sandbar grew narrower and narrower until finally you could walk to the sandbar at low tide.

Seventy Thousand cubic yards of sand build up Sandy Point every year, then bypass the mouth of Plum Island Sound and build up Crane's Beach. This all happens to the delight of Ipswichites, the consternation of Plum Island residents and the total indifference of Mother Nature.

CHAPTER 2
Fish Crows
August 6, 2017

Fish Crow near Plum Island Point Lighthouse.

On August 6, 2017 I led a group of citizen scientists to the Merrimack River's south jetty, where a flock of shorebirds were sitting on the sand waiting for the tide to go out. I excused my ignorance of ornithology by making a lame joke along the lines that marine biologists separate their birds into big brown birds, little brown birds and owls. But I did recognize some Fish Crows amongst the black backed seagulls picking through the detritus of last night's storm.

I didn't recognize Fish Crows the first time I saw them squabbling in the pine trees on Plum Island Point. But I found myself instantly transposed to Florida by their calls. The winter before, I had watched a flock of them making a ruckus around a swimming pool in Boca Grande.

One crow was the rock star of the flock. He had discovered that if he sat inside a curved brick cupola covering the pool house chimney his calls would be amplified so he could dominate his confrères and attract females.

I had lived in Massachusetts all my life and seen lots of American crows including two I had raised as chicks. They used to live in the trees around our house and whenever someone came out of the house, the crows would fly down, land on their shoulders and start begging for food.

But I had never seen Fish Crows either inland or on Cape Cod because they live around the mouths of fresh water rivers. Like turkey vultures and cardinals they have only recently moved this far north due to global warming. In fact the Merrimack River is now about the northernmost extent of their range.

The amazing thing about Fish Crows is how little research has been done on them. About the only thing you can find is how to tell them apart from American crows. The only sure way to do it is through their calls.

American crows have the distinct "caw, caw" cry that we are used to. Fish Crows have a more nasal call. One ornithologist wrote that the best way to tell the birds apart is to ask a crow if he is an American Crow. If he answers "uh, uh" it is a Fish Crow. Another birder pointed out that Fish Crows sound like American crows but with Boston accents. No doubt this is true because a Fish Crow is definitely smarter than your average American crow.

Plum Island's Fish crows are particularly smart and gregarious. They know the social rank of all the other birds in their flock and even seem to recognize the leaders of other groups they often join on common foraging grounds. I suppose it is a little like our knowing the names of leaders of other countries we have to live with on this crowded planet of ours.

All Corvids are intelligent. Ravens will lead a pack of wolves to a carcass and the wolves will then open the body and let the ravens get to the good parts. Then, while the wolves are busy feasting the ravens will keep an eye out for competing predators because they have much better eyesight than the wolves.

The Inuit believe that ravens lead them to prey by dipping their wings in their direction, but raven have also been known to pull unattended fishing lines up through the ice in order to steal a fisherman's catch. And humans have yet to devise a trashcan ravens can't burglarize.

But fortunately our Fish Crows were reasonably well behaved and made charming additions to the fauna of Plum Island Point.

CHAPTER 3
Blue Mussels, Red Tide
August 12, 2017

Blue Mussels, Red Tide. Blue Mussels.

On August 12, 2017 I checked my tide table and called the shellfish warden's line for his recorded report on the state of shellfish beds in the town of Ipswich. Most of the clam flats were open but all the mussel beds in the town were closed. I didn't think too much about the final announcement. We had had several days of rain so the E-coli counts were probably high.

But I had been weathering some oyster shells in my backyard and wanted to return them to the water so more spat could settle on the shells. And since I would be at Eagle Hill anyway, I decided to continue to the mussel beds to take a look for myself.

When I arrived I saw a guy scraping mussels off the rocks. I called out to him to explain that the beds were closed but he didn't seem to hear. Since I didn't have anything else to do I decided to walk out to the beds to get his attention. He didn't speak English very well so I used pantomime to try to explain that he could get sick from eating the mussels. He said, "OK" but went back to his work.

I figured I had done my part and decided not to press the point. But a few days later a neighbor told me that the state had closed all the mussels' beds in the commonwealth because of red tide. Had I known I would have used much more graphic pantomime and perhaps have even had the shellfish warden warn the gentleman. Eating contaminated clams is one thing, eating mussels with red tide is a whole different kettle of fish.

Red tides are caused by tiny Gonyaulax dinoflagellates that spend most of their lives as inanimate cysts encased in mud. But excessive rainfall can cause the cysts to open and the red tide organisms to bloom, often turning coastal waters reddish pink with their abundance. On the West Coast, Native Americans used to set up sentries to warn of such red tides.

Mussels are the first shellfish to pick up the dinoflagellates because they filter food more efficiently than other shellfish. So the state tests mussels on a regular basis and when they find that the number of red tide organisms rises above 80 parts per million they close down the beds.

But then towns have a problem like the one facing Amityville in the movie *Jaws*. If they mention the word red tide or even the more technical term paralytic shellfish poisoning people will stop eating all species of clams and fishermen will lose income during their make it or break it summer season. But only blue mussels may have exceeded the official limit.

But the likelihood remains that someone won't get the word and become sick and even die from eating affected mussels.

After all, paralytic shellfish poison is dangerous stuff. Years ago a Bulgarian diplomat was getting off a bus in London when a man jostled him with an umbrella. The diplomat died a few hours later of what was initially thought to be from a heart attack. But when officials exhumed the body several months later they discovered a tiny metal sphere filled with paralytic shellfish poison that had been injected into the diplomat's neck when his assassin jostled him.

Hopefully nobody will start injecting themselves with paralytic shellfish poison, but perhaps we should start taking a more precautionary approach in deciding whether or not to announce that blue mussels have been afflicted with red tide organisms.

CHAPTER 4
Revival
August 13, 2017

Catching Schoolies off Plum Island Point.

On August 13, I took an ecological group around Plum Island Point to check on the fishing season. The mouth of the Merrimack River is one of the best places on the East Coast to catch striped bass because they lie in deep holes in easy casting distance, and lunge out at baitfish disoriented by the intermixing of fresh and salt water.

In June there were over a hundred fishermen lined up along this shore catching fourteen to twenty inch "schoolies." Now there were fewer fishermen but they were catching larger fish between 25 and 30 inches. By regulation, the fish had to be 28 inches long or more to be "keepers" .

The same thing was happening up and down the East Coast. Millions of schoolies had emerged from their nursery grounds in Chesapeake Bay, then spread from Maryland to Maine. The mature fish had migrated in from offshore.

The mature fish had hatched in 2011 so they were from the so-called 2011 year class, a solidly productive year. The immature schoolies were from the much larger 2014 and 2015 year classes. But there were no fish between 20 and 25 inches, because so few fish hatched out in 2012 and 2013. So the interesting question is why were 2011, 2014 and 2015 such good years and 2012 and 2013 such bad years?

The reason could lie in the amount of rain that fell during those years. It turns out that larval striped bass are particularly susceptible to acid rain. In the Seventies, scientists discovered that Spring storms would wash pulses of acid rain into the Chesapeake where they killed off large numbers of larval fish.

Today, reports of precipitation in the Chesapeake from 2011 to 2015 are equivocal but suggestive. It could be that acid rain is still a problem even though regulations cut back sulphur emissions from power plants. Or it could be that years with high precipitation water down pollution. We don't know the answer but it probably lies in recent climatic and meteorological changes.

What we do know is that this has been the best summer for catching striped bass in over 15 years. When the schoolies start to mature and spawn, each fish can produce up to four million eggs. So the 2014 and 2015 year classes could pass through the population like a pig in a python spawning succeeding generations.

Seeing people catching the mature fish from the 2011 year is more problematic because the fish hatched in 2011 are now the prime spawners, but several fishermen told me they were releasing the larger fish to preserve the population. Hopefully officials will raise the size limit for keepers to protect these year classes as well.

But one concern is what all these fish are feeding on. Normally they would be chowing down on menhaden but in recent years hundreds of tons of menhaden have been scooped up by purse seiners and processed for the Omega-3 fish pill industry. Many of the schoolies do look scrawny and many dawdled in the Chesapeake where they could find more available food.

And then of course there is the recent phenomenon of Great White Sharks. Charter boat captains report that dozens of them lurk in Cape Cod Bay waiting for the boats to hook a striped bass, then the sharks leap entirely out of the water to chop the bass in two.

The fishermen go home with great stories, but somehow it doesn't seem too sporting of the predators on either end of the fishing line.

CHAPTER 5
Eclipse
August 21, 2017

"May the Shadow of the Moon Fall on a World at Peace."
- Frank Reynolds
ABC News
February 26, 1979

Watching the eclipse from our back yard in Ipswich.

OK I'll admit it. I'm an eclipse snob. The first one I experienced was on a canoe trip in Northern Quebec. We hadn't seen another human being for two months, and we were crossing Lake Mistassini, which is a hundred miles long and thirty miles wide. The lake was like a mirror reflecting the gray sky above and the gray water below. We couldn't see the horizon and we couldn't see land. We felt like we were suspended in a void of never ending gray.

Each canoe had a husky puppy in its bow, and suddenly all of them raised their snouts and started howling. The temperature dropped and it became noticeably darker. Nobody knew what was happening. Nobody said anything. We just paddled a little harder in order to reach the far shore before the weather changed.

I was bent over, pulling on my paddle, when I noticed that something was missing from the reflection of the sun traveling in the water beside us. It finally hit me. We were in an eclipse and it felt like the end of the world.

My second eclipse occurred in February 1979. I had loaded four friends from college in my family's flimsy aluminum skiff and we motored 12 miles down Cape Cod's Pleasant Bay and across to Monomoy Island. Monomoy was the only place in the entire United States that was going to experience totality.

The shoreline looked like a pilgrimage. Thousands of people dressed in long robes and colorful hippie garb walked slowly down the beach as if to Finisterre. Chatham's finest were busy arresting people who had commandeered old tin tubs to cross the cold currents of the dangerous passage. For good measure they had also tossed the entire Harvard band into the hoosegow for repeatedly playing the theme from "2001" at the end of the desolate beach.

It started to get very dark. The entire horizon looked like sunset, then totality occurred and the stars and planets came out as quickly as if someone had turned down a rheostat. Seagulls flew in to roost, looking in the direction of the sun and bands of light, the so-called snakes in the grass, rippled up and down the length of the beach. On the way home it looked like the heads of seals were poking through clouds, but the clouds were being reflected on the surface of the water.

So I didn't expect much from the August 21 eclipse. It seemed too overhyped and commercialized so I decided to just do some errands and listen to reports from small towns and cities in the 60 mile wide path of totality as the eclipse swept from Oregon to South Carolina.

It was the first time an eclipse had crossed over our entire country since 1918. The time before that, John Adams had damaged his eyes from staring at the sun from the top of Beacon Hill.

Hundreds of thousands of people had flocked to high school football fields, small museums and community college campuses. They had come from all over the world and spent the night in tents, campers and trailers.

A hush fell over some groups, others broke into cheers. There was usually a scientist in each group excitedly reporting on the appearance of Bailey's Beads, the diamond affect and coronal storms. A beagle just wagged his tail in Oregon but thousands of cicada emerged to chirr in the inky darkness over Nashville.

One final photo showed half a dozen White House aides clad in eclipse glasses staring at the sun from the Truman balcony. It looked like a scene from Independence Day.

Yet it was perhaps the first time in history that our country was united in wonder at our place in the natural world. And we didn't even have to fire off a rocket to make the event happen.

CHAPTER 6
Lessons From Harvey
August 25, 2017

Hurricane Harvey- courtesy Inside Business.

In late August the world was transfixed by stories, both heart wrenching and heart warming, as Hurricane Harvey threw down its wrath on the lowlands of Texas and Louisiana. The best thing to come out of this vengeful storm could be for cities like Newburyport to learn from the decisions, made by Houston and surrounding communities.

THE STORM

First we should investigate what caused this particular storm. For the first time in recorded history the temperature of the surface waters of the Gulf of Mexico had not dipped below 73 degrees all winter.

By August, the Gulf was an 86 degree superheated cauldron of latent energy that fueled the rapid acceleration of Harvey from a run of the mill tropical storm to a Cat 4 hurricane — a hurricane with rain bands that dumped over 50 inches of rain on an area the size of New York City and Chicago combined, or enough water to fill a cube 2 miles high, by 2 miles long by 2 miles wide.

It would be scientific reticence, if not scientific malfeasance to repeat the old saw that no individual storm can be definitively based on climate change. But, this was the third 500-year storm to hit the area in the last three years. And even though there were no major storms in 2016, flooding was so severe that the year went down as the third most costly year in history for disaster relief. So the first lesson that Harvey can teach us is that the climate is now brewing bigger storms, causing more frequent and intense flooding.

BARRIER BEACHES

Newburyport can learn a second lesson from Hurricane Harvey- if you are fortunate enough to have a barrier beach protecting your city, for gosh sakes take care of it. It is your first line of defense. If you didn't already have it, you would have to build a storm surge barrier for close to a billion bucks.

Don't weaken your barrier with groinfields that create hotspots of erosion. Don't build seawalls that increase that erosion and fail every year, and don't alter jetties to cause new areas of erosion on your precious barrier island.

EVACUATIONS

The third lesson we can learn is to make judicious decisions about evacuating in the event of a major storm. It makes sense to urge people to evacuate from barrier islands before they get cut off from both escape and first responders.

But think carefully about urging people to evacuate a major city. Houston would have had to evacuate 4.5 million people and it would have made matters worse to have all of them stuck in their cars in the two hundred mile area that was flooded. It would have lead to the same often fatal, multiday traffic jam that happened when New Orleans tried to evacuate its population before Hurricane Rita.

RESILIENCY

The fourth lesson is to make private homes and public infrastructure more resilient. Much of the flooding was exacerbated because Houston had been sprawling willy-nilly across the landscape for decades. In doing so it had built hundreds of thousands of acres of impermeable roads and parking lots that increased run-off into streets that lacked adequate drainage in the first place. Storm surge in the Houston waterway also prevented the run-off water from draining down into the harbor and adjoining ocean.

The same Obama era construction regulations that President Trump had rescinded two weeks before the storm would have prevented the construction of equally flood prone homes that will probably be built after this storm passes.

THE EPA

The explosions at the Arkema chemical plant in Crosby, Texas highlighted the importance of EPA regulations that would have required that the French owned company have a backup to their refrigeration system.

The company should have had a compound on hand that would have inactivated their organic peroxides. But the compound would have also made their peroxides unsalable, so the company had turned to the Texas Congressional delegation to have the regulation delayed until President Trump was in office.

COMING TOGETHER

What Houston did most admirably was to unite in the face of this crisis. It didn't matter if people were black, white, rich, poor documented or not. Everyone was literally in the same boat, whether being rescued or helping to rescue others. And, if we learned anything from rebuilding New Orleans, foreign labor (both documented and undocumented) would be needed to rebuild Houston.

HUMILITY IN THE FACE OF NATURE

But perhaps the most amazing thing that Harvey accomplished was to humble our president who had been watching the news incessantly as was his want. Somebody must have also been handling him very carefully because for the most part our instinct driven president got it right, offering aid and comfort and staying out of the way of professionals who had crucial jobs to perform.

CHAPTER 7
The Residents' Cruise
September 2, 2017

The residents cruise in the Merrimack River.

The day after Hurricanes Katrina and Sandy made landfall it was obvious that they were major tragedies. That had not been the case with Hurricane Harvey. Its initial winds had caused some immediate damage but it was the relentless rains that caused the ongoing flooding, broken dams, overtopped levees and toxic spills. These differences were to have important consequences for both homeowners and the Federal Flood Insurance Program that was up for reauthorization on September 31.

It took more than a week for many people in Houston to realize that they had only been covered for wind damage. Their houses had not been in designated flood plain areas, so they had never been told about flood insurance because their banks didn't require it in order to purchase their mortgages.

This meant that many of Houston's 100,000 damaged homes would sit in muddy waters and be filled with smelly mold for days on end. And even owners who did have flood insurance faced spending months wading through red tape as their houses rotted from within. Only a fortunate few would have the resources on hand to immediately start stripping and rebuilding their homes.

On September 2, I used the occasion of a delightful cruise to start researching how many people on Plum Island were covered by flood insurance.

It was the second year that George Charos had offered this sunset cruise to his neighbors and about 60 people had showed up. His spotless whale watching boat wended its way up the Merrimack River through hordes of Labor Day boaters out on the harbor to watch the Newburyport's Riverfest music festival.

I felt like Debbie Downer bringing up flood insurance as summer people were happily catching up with winter people and enjoying platters of food made from their neighbors' favorite recipes. But storms were on everyone's minds. We had all watched the tragedy unfold in Texas and Hurricane Irma was lumbering toward the East Coast. Weather forecasters had even started warning New Englanders to haul in their boats, stoke up on food and stow their outside furniture under cover.

What I discovered was that very few people knew much about the Federal Flood Insurance Program. I had only recently found out myself that the reason my family didn't have flood insurance on a house only 52 feet from the water was that it sat on a 30 foot high bluff, therefore it was not considered to be in a flood plain.

I soon learned that Plum Island, like Houston, had a hop scotch pattern of coverage. But there was no central agency where you could easily find the information, so in the event of a storm like Harvey it would only be after the fact that local officials would find out who had been covered and who had not been.

The entire oceanfront of Plum Island and much of the backshore is considered to be in a flood zone, so most of those houses are covered under the federal program. But most of the people who had paid cash to rebuild houses on the footprints of houses destroyed by storms, like the one in March 2013, were not covered because they didn't have mortgages.

Some houses were "grandfathered" in because the former owners of their homes had bought mortgages before the requirement had gone into effect. Others lay on the thin strip of highland that forms the backbone of the island and is not considered to be in a flood zone.

So if a major storm hit Plum Island tomorrow it would take weeks to discover who was covered and who was not, and if owners found they were covered they could only collect $250,000 for damage to their homes and not to damage to their lots which were often more valuable than their houses.

This spotty coverage shows the great weakness of the program. The entire island is vulnerable but only some of the residents are required to carry flood insurance so there are not enough premiums to cover the overall risk. Compound that across the country where only people who live on rivers and along the coast pay premiums for flood insurance and you can see why the federal Flood Insurance is $25 Billion dollars in debt. That would be the political football Congress would have to tackle when it had to vote to reform the system by September 31.

CHAPTER 8
Hurricanes, Gundalows and Northeasters
September 7, 2017

Gundalow entering Newburyport Harbor.

On September 7, I spent the day exploring the length and breadth of Plum Island. I started at the south end of the island, where flocks of tree swallows were gathering to start their winter migrations. Thousands of them flitted through the dunegrass and deftly caught mosquitoes buzzing over the tidepool at the terminus of the island.

The tide was racing through the narrow inlet to the tidepool and I paused to watch dollops of sand plop into the rushing waters as they eroded the overhanging dune. A pair of dowitchers dunked their long thin bills in and out of the tidepool, driving schools of minnows to distraction.

I took special note of the recurving sandbar that had created this long thin pool about the length and width of 3 football fields. Sprouts of Spartina salt marsh hay were already thriving in the shallow end of the pool and when dunegrass started to colonize the sandbar it would help raise its elevation enough for bayberry and cedar trees to take root

But it was getting late and I had made plans to take a historic cruise on the Merrimack River. As the boat approached its lateen sails made it look like something you would expect to see plying the Nile, for this was a replica of a gundalow. Gundalows used to be the workhorse boats of the Merrimack and Piscataqua Rivers. And this would be the first time in over a hundred years that such a barge had sailed these waters.

In colonial times, their owners used tidal power to transport their gundalows up and down the rivers. They would load their boats upriver at high tide, then let the outgoing tide sweep them to the mouth of the river many miles downstream. Then, they would reverse the process and load their boats with cargo from downriver and let the incoming tide carry them to upriver ports.

It would only take one or two men to steer the barges down the river with long thin sweeping oars or they might use poles to pole the gundalows through places like Plum Island Sound. It was not really very hard work. I imagine the crew caught quite a few fish as they drifted quietly down the river.

At this time of year the gundalows would have been piled high with stacks of salt marsh hay on the first leg of their trip to Hay Market Square in Boston. In later years the owners added square sails and lateen sails to make their gundalows faster. The lateen rig provided an added benefit; its main mast could be easily folded back so the boat could glide under the low bridges that had started to span the Merrimack and Piscataqua Rivers.

Our gundalow was so quiet and low in the water that it made me realize how wide the mouth of the Merrimack River really was, and how fast it flowed as it was forced between the jetties into the Atlantic Ocean.

I met two birders on the cruise who invited me to go back to the center of the island at sunset to watch immature gannets as they tucked in their wings and plunged 30 feet below the surface to catch baitfish. But soon our shadows were growing longer and longer on the beach and we left as the surf lapped quietly on the now empty shore.

A few days later the chassis of old cars started to appear on the beach below the remains of the Old Coast Guard Station on the north end of the island. It was the signal that the 2018 erosion season was about to really begin. Since June, waves had been incrementally adding more sand to the beach than they had been eroding. This had made the beach about four feet deeper than it was during the winter. But now more energy was causing the reverse. Each wave was taking a little more sand off the beach than it was depositing so the shore was starting to erode.

But it didn't quite seem fair that we were enjoying such perfect weather while Hurricane Irma was bearing down on Florida. It was equally unsettling to realize that even though the chances of such a storm making a direct hit on Plum Island were relatively low, if it did, almost every house and all the island's infrastructure would be destroyed.

Such a hurricane would have to by-pass Cape Cod then make an abrupt turn to the west as Sandy had done off New Jersey. However, we had a more pressing concern. While Florida is more likely to get hit by a hurricane than any other state, Massachusetts is more likely to get hit by a major storm. This is because we have all these pesky little Northeasters that cause so much erosion because they stick around through several tidal cycles and they would soon be on their way!

CHAPTER 9
Humpbacks and Hurricanes
September 15, 2017

Humpback whale feeding just offshore. Sandy Tilton photo.

September 15 was a hazy, hot, end-of-summer day. A seal watched curiously as a man waved his towel overhead, and flocks of herring gulls flew in front of tall white cumulus clouds. Three people silhouetted in the fog stood at the water's edge aiming their smart phones at the empty ocean.

Then it happened. A school of fusiform bodies exploded out of the water followed by the immense open jaws of a humpback whale. Menhaden cascaded out of its great maw as the giant gulped down half a ton of the silvery, foot-long fish.

We were enveloped in a smelly miasma of fish oil and humpback halitosis. It took me awhile to realize that we were so close to the whales we were actually smelling their odiferous breath.

The only time I had been this close to a whale, I was in an eighteen-foot Boston Whaler off Provincetown, Massachusetts. Apparently the finback whale we had been following had gone to sleep under our boat because when we started the engine it rose right beside us and our boat lurched down into the hole it created. I ended up holding my camera overhead wondering if I could swim to shore. Fortunately the boat righted itself and I didn't have to discover if I could swim a quarter of a mile with one of my arms out of water.

Tuna, gray seals, harbor seals, and long, thin Minke whales that looked like miniature blue whales were also feeding on the menhaden. The menhaden were an encouraging sign. In recent years tons upon tons of the prolific fish had been swept out of the oceans for the Omega-3 fish pill industry.

In aerial photos the schools of menhaden were so massive they looked like clouds and the whales looked only like tiny dots. You could also see how effective these plankton eating fish really were. The water in front of the schools was dark with plankton while the water behind them schools was clear.

Apparently the ocean was so hot the menhaden had migrated this far north, and our recent spate of hurricanes had pushed the schools close to shore, where at least one of their flanks was protected. It was also more difficult for the whales to capture the menhaden because the water was less than thirty feet deep.

And now the menhaden were trapped by the Merrimack River's North Jetty. It would be interesting to see if the whales would follow the menhaden around the jetties as they continued their migrations south.

CHAPTER 10
The $24 Million Dollar Mistake
September 20, 2018

The $24 Million dollar mistake.

September 20 was a cool, blustery day. Hurricanes Harvey and Irma had just decimated Texas and Florida and now it looked like Jose was going to sit south of Nantucket spinning off storm surges and long period waves for several days. But nobody was complaining. The longer Jose persisted the more likely it was that hurricane Maria would stay offshore saving New England from a direct hit.

Goldenrod glistened in the drizzly light rain and kite surfers slashed back and forth along North Point Beach as four-foot high waves undercut her dunes. Hopefully this storm would be a wake-up call for the government officials who had dropped the ball after protecting the houses on Northern Reservation Terrace last spring.

The problem had started, as it often does, with a lack of adequate science. In this case people had been told that longshore currents push sand primarily south along this section of Plum Island. Actually waves hit the center of the island from the East, which sets up longshore currents that push sand from the center of the island north and from the center of the island south. So where should you build a house on such an island? On the growing ends, or in the eroding middle?

The homeowners in the center of the island had hired a high priced lobbyist that used erroneous science to convince the Army Corps of Engineers to repair the Merrimack River's south jetty. This was all done in the mistaken belief that repairing the jetty would stop erosion in front of their houses in Newbury, more than a mile away.

So, I walked to the top of the jetty to take a closer look at this $24 million dollar mistake. The Corps had essentially built a 30-foot high dam that was holding back about a million cubic yards of sand—sand that wanted to flow naturally around the point to build up the beach in front of the homes on Northern Reservation Terrace.

Four years ago, these houses sat behind 400 feet of well-vegetated dunes. Since the jetty had been repaired the beach had been eroding at the rate of 150 feet a year or about 30 feet during the stormy winter months. And Hurricane Jose was giving us a taste of what those winter months would be like.

Seven-foot waves riding on top of a nine-foot high tide were sweeping fishermen off their feet and pounding the jetty from both sides. The waves had already created a ridge of sand along the shore and a runnel behind the ridge where water from the waves would rush several hundred feet down the beach carrying a great slurry of sand that was washing over and through the jetty to the other side.

Each wave had enough force to liquefy the sand under the jetty and jiggle the multi-ton boulders so they had settled into the underlying sand. This process had caused the jetty to settle two and a half feet since 2014.

It would only take a few more storms like Hurricane Jose to lower the jetty enough so that more sand was flowing onto the beach than eroding off of it. The same thing had happened after the jetty had been repaired in the Sixties when it had settled almost 4 feet during the 1978 Blizzard alone.

So now we were in a race to see whether the jetty would settle enough for the beach to start growing or whether the ocean would start undermining the houses on Northern Reservation Terrace less than 40 feet away. And it was clear that the upcoming winter would decide which would happen first. Last year the state had built a $150,000 sacrificial dune system that had slowed the rate of erosion from 150 feet a year to about 75 feet a year.

If someone could find the money to do the same thing this year it could give Nature just enough time to repair the $24 million dollar mistake. We would know more when the Merrimack River Beach Alliance met on September 29.

CHAPTER 11
The Proposal
September 24, 2017

Measuring erosion on Plum Island Point. Sandy Tilton photo.

It's surprisingly difficult to judge how much a beach has eroded after a storm. You can see that waves have cut back the dunes, but it is hard to know whether they have eroded back two feet, or five feet, or ten feet.

I received a striking example of this phenomenon when I was driving down to Chatham every month to photograph erosion. I arrived one day and found that the beach looked exactly like it had the month before. But then I realized there used to be a house on the same spot. The beach had simply eroded sixty feet back and repaired itself so it looked like a natural beach once again.

To avoid making this kind of mistake, I brought a group of citizen scientists to the end of Plum Island's North Point to take hand measurements of erosion at the end of a boardwalk that leads to the beach. It looked like the dune had only eroded back five or six feet, but when we measured the featureless dune we discovered it had eroded back 22 feet since August 3rd. And most of that erosion had occurred during the past week when long period waves from Hurricane Jose had been pounding this shore.

The amount of erosion was significant because the residents of Northern Reservation Terrace were floating the idea of putting $2 collected from the Plum Island Point parking lot's regular $12 fee into a fund dedicated to protecting the dunes.

Inevitably, a small group of people took an instant dislike to the idea, claiming that it made the beach less public than before. Many of the same people had railed against having the state mark off a few designated pathways to the beach, rather than having people trample through the dunes on 17 random paths that had grown up haphazardly over the past thirty odd years.

But nobody had complained about the paths during the summer, and most found that the Mobi-mats the state had supplied made it much easier to walk safely through the fragile dunes.

But our measurement showed that by 2019 the question would be moot. At the present rate of erosion, there wasn't going to be any beach to walk on. The ocean would be lapping at the wall in front of the houses on Northern Reservation Terrace and along the Plum Island Point parking lot.

There would be no sand to lie on, no shore to fish from and no dunes to walk through. So a two-dollar fee to help rebuild the dunes didn't seem too excessive to avoid this eminently avoidable public loss.

CHAPTER 12
The Meeting
September 29, 2017

PITA Hall.

The Merrimack River Beach User's Alliance held its monthly meeting on September 29. The intergovernmental group had been delayed all summer because its chairman had several recalcitrant kidney stones. Hopefully the meeting would prove to be less painful.

I have a theory that the less meetings you hold, the more people will attend them. This proved to be the case. PITA Hall was packed with residents, government officials and the press.

The meeting started off with a shock. The Army Corps of Engineer's Ed O'Donnell announced that their so-called DOTS study had determined that the Corp's jetty had not caused erosion in front of Northern Reservation Terrace.

This was at odds with common sense as well as all the most recent research. Even Ed seemed a little embarrassed by the conclusion, stressing that the Corp's employees had only flown up from their offices in Mississippi for a few days to take a cursory look at old data.

Apparently it was long enough for them to come up with the idea that the 350 feet of erosion that we had measured since 2015 had been caused by a natural cycle. It was clear that this was primarily a political document that the Corps hoped would forestall their having to undertake a more rigorous Section 111 study. If that study determined the Corps was at fault it could be on the hook to fix the problem for up to $10 million dollars.

It was noteworthy that the report's cycle of twenty to thirty years of natural erosion came suspiciously close to matching the cycle of erosion and growth that had occurred when the jetties had been repaired in 1970, then again in 2012 — a convenient coincidence to be sure.

Ed's report was followed with a modeling study done by GZA, the company that had designed the system of sacrificial dunes that had slowed the rate of erosion from 150 feet a year to 75 feet a year in 2017. Needless to say their study refuted the Corp's DOTS study, as had a study done by Woods Hole in 2016 and another done for the Corps by Dennis Hubbard in the Seventies.

After continuing on and on about everything that had to be done to get the Corps to dump sand from the Pisquatiqua River in Maine and the Merrimack River either on to the beach or offshore, the meeting finally arrived at new business, the creation of a Northern Reservation Terrace Subcommittee to decide what could be done to prevent houses from being washed away in the next few months.

This had been the problem all along. Instead of focusing on the immediate issue, officials had become so enmeshed in the red tape involved with getting sand in the future they had dropped the ball about addressing the coming winter's erosion.

Fortunately, Mayor Donna Holaday of Newburyport was at the meeting. I had the distinct feeling that she was open to the idea of having one person in her administration in charge of saving the houses, beach and infrastructure of Northern Reservation Terrace and finding money for the long-term maintenance of the dunes.

Funds could come through fees collected from parking lots on the island and perhaps from a betterment or from parking lots in the city itself. This meant that the residents of Northern Reservation Terrace would have to appear before the Newburyport City Council in the very near future.

CHAPTER 13
Erosion or a Loss of Accretion?
Plum Island Point
October 8, 2017

Long period wave riding up on the wing bar to crash into the high dune area.

On October 8, I drove to Plum Island to figure out exactly how waves and the South Jetty were eroding the beach in front of Northern Reservation Terrace.

The first thing I noticed was a set of four or five foot high waves hitting South Jetty from the north. This made sense. The waves were coming from the NorthEast. But the north jetty should be blocking them. Were they somehow reforming after breaking over the jetty?

Then I noticed that another set of four or five foot waves were hitting the inside of North Jetty and traveling along it rapidly into the river mouth. This didn't make sense if the waves were coming from the Northeast.

Next I noticed a third set of eight foot waves that seemed to rise up out of nowhere and crash into dunes near the Plum Island Point boardwalk.

Finally I saw four or five foot waves attacking the dunes along a wide arc of the beach in front of Northern Reservation Terrace. During all this time, the waves in center of the mouth of river were barely perceptible, less than foot high and not breaking.

The first hint I had of what was going on was when I realized that at sea these long period waves had been hardly high enough to be felt on a boat. It was only when they approached the shore that friction from the bottom caused the lower half of the waves to slow, causing the upper half of the waves to rise to their full height and break against the shore like a miniature tsunami.

So a 20 foot long period wave might only be a foot high at sea, but then rise up to about 8 feet and break when it rode up on the wing bar that projects several hundred feet into the mouth of the Merrimack River.

All this had come together when Dan Stapleton from GZA showed me an old photograph of the physical model of the mouth of the river. The Corps used to make these models for every river they planned to dredge.

You could see an engineer standing on the model that was perfect in every detail and took up several hundred feet of floor space in the Corp's old modeling lab in Vicksburg Mississippi.

The model revealed that when long period waves entered the river from the ocean, they had to squeeze through the jetties. Then they would expand and arc across the mouth of the river about a quarter of a mile from one side to the other.

So the waves that struck the inside of the South Jetty were from the southern end of the elongated waves and the set of waves that hit the inside of the North Jetty were from the northern end of these curved waves that were breaking in a wide arc along the entire length of the Plum Island Point Shore.

So this was the process that eroded about 150 feet off Plum Island Point every year. But under normal conditions this baseline erosion would be replaced by about 155 feet of accretion, so the net growth of the beach would be a few feet per year. But, since the jetty had been repaired this accretion has not been able to override the erosion on Plum Island Point.

The bottom line of all this, is that it is more accurate to say the problem caused by repairing South Jetty is not so much erosion, but the loss of accretion in front of the houses on Northern Reservation Terrace.

CHAPTER 14
The Cove
October 10, 2017

The type of dredge that could scoop sand out of the cove and spray it on the dunes.
Courtesy Elliot dredge.

On October 10, I took advantage of our extended Indian Summer to investigate a shallow cove created by waves sweeping around the spur of the jetty in front of Northern Reservation Terrace. Our group of citizen scientist photographers had been keeping track of a four-foot high pipe that juts out of the sand at the edge of the cove.

In the winter, the pipe was fully exposed and you could see that it turned and snaked back horizontally to the remains of the old Coast Guard Station. The pipe was probably the top of a chain link fence that used to surround the station.

In the summer the pipe was often completely covered with sand. This showed that the summer beach was at least 4 feet deeper than the winter beach. The sand that built up this beach was constantly being replaced by sand flowing through the jetty and coming to a temporary rest in the cove.

We have another way of determining how much the beach changes during the year. Last year, a piece of timber from the remains of the station jutted out of the dune. In the summer you could almost touch it, in the winter it was 10 feet over your head.

Fortunately, this source of sand lay close to where the state built its sacrificial sand dune system the year before. The state had used sand dredged from beneath George Charos' *Captain's Lady's* dock at the end of Plum Island Point. George had to dredge the sand out of the river, then the state had to load it into trucks, deliver it to Olga Way, then deliver to the dual dune system, all for the tune of about $150,000.

This sand could simply be pumped inexpensively out of the cove and sprayed directly on the nearby dune. There are several types of dredges that could do this. One would be a lawn mower sized dredge similar to the one George Charos used. It could either be operated from the deck of a small boat floating in the cove, or it could be run from the bucket of a Bob Cat on the beach.

Someone on the boat or in waders could skim the intake pipe over the bottom so it would only suck up a few inches of sand and water that would be pumped through a pipe to the top of the dune. A secondary pump and pipe would spray the slurry back and forth to create layers of sand.

What you would be doing is mimicking what happens during winter storms, when waves overtop the dunes and deposit up to a foot of sand on top of the dormant dune grass. The dune grass then grows up through the sand leaving behind a thick matrix of rhizomes to bind the dune together internally.

Of course you would need city, state and Army Corps of Engineer's permits but those should be forthcoming. Hopefully the Merrimack River Beach Alliance would concentrate officials' attention on this unique opportunity to work with nature and solve a problem caused by working against nature with multi-ton boulders and jetties.

CHAPTER 15
Two Bombshells
October 20, 2017

Building seawalls.

The Merrimack River Beach Alliance held its October meeting on the 20th. Most of the meeting was taken up with discussing the same old problem, what still had to be done to get dredge spoils from the Piscataqua River to Plum Island.

Bob Boeri, from the state's Coastal Zone Management Office stressed that state agencies and local communities had to start applying for permits right away to meet the fast approaching deadlines. As an added inducement, he also mentioned that the town of Hull was much further along in the process than Newbury, Newburyport and Salisbury.

Representative Lenny Meara agreed to head up a sub-committee to look into dredges that the state or Essex County could purchase so they would have access to their own sources of sand without having to rely on the Army Corps of Engineers.

That was when the Corp's Ed O'Donnell dropped the first bombshell. The Corps had decided that sand from the Piscataqua River would not be deposited off Newburyport, but off Newbury. Apparently the Corps had made the decision internally without any scientific scrutiny or doing a cost benefit analysis. Perhaps Newbury's homeowners had convinced them that the houses in Newbury were in greater danger than the houses in Newburyport's Northern Reservation Terrace area.

If the recent spate of hurricanes has taught us anything it is that if people want to continue living on barrier beach islands they will have to start making difficult decisions based on science and economics rather than facile decisions based on politics alone.

The harsh reality was that nothing had worked or would work to make Newbury's first tier house in the center of the island safer. The groins had simply opened holes in the offshore sandbar creating hotspots of erosion.

The illegal seawalls had failed every year since they had been built in 2013 and repairing the south jetty had put 250 homes at risk in Newburyport while not doing anything to help the houses in Newbury a mile away.

If sand were placed off Newbury the groins would simply reopen the holes in the sandbars recreating the hotspots of erosion. But if the sand were placed in the originally permitted site off Newburyport, it would flow through the jetty the following winter and the beach and dunes would start growing in front of the homes on Northern Reservation Terrace again.

Then the city of Newburyport dropped its own bombshell. It had discovered between 40 and 60 truckfulls of sand that had washed onto George Charos' parking lot. The officials were excited that the sand could be used to rebuild the sacrificial dunes in front of Northern Reservation that were only a few hundred yards away. Bob Boeri was quick to dampen that excitement by pointing out that the city would have to get permits to both remove the sand and place it in the dunes.

Bob's caution highlighted an irony in the one-size fits all permitting process. It is relatively easy to get permission to dredge sand out of the Merrimack River, where it is considered to be a hazard to navigation, but if that same sand washes onto a beach or into sand dunes it is considered to be part of the barrier beach system protected by the state's wetlands protection act.

But the situation had revealed just how much sand had accumulated on Plum Island's North Point. Much of it had been deposited there between 2009, when the Corps had pumped sand onto the center of the island, and 2012, when the south jetty repair had cut down the flow of sand from about 70,000 cubic yards to about 30,000 cubic yards of sand per year. Now all that sand was sitting at the end of Plum Island Point in several long thick sandbars projecting into the river.

It was clear that there was a great deal of sand that had flowed out of the sediment transport system and was now sitting in what coastal geologists call sand sinks.

In terms of a cost benefit analysis, the costs of dumping sand off Newbury would be about $3.5 Million dollars and the benefit would be nil. But the cost of using sand from local sand sinks to rebuild the sacrificial dunes would be about $150,000 and the benefit would be to protect the 250 homes on Northern Reservation Terrace worth at least $125 Million dollars, a pretty positive ratio in my book.

CHAPTER 16
The Puerto Rico Experiment
October 25, 2017

The first thing Virgin Air's Richard Branson noticed when he crawled out of his cellar after Hurricane Irma was the solar array. It lay on the ground unharmed while his Caribbean home and everything surrounding it had been totally destroyed. People noticed the same thing in Haiti and Florida. Hurricane Harvey had snapped the power lines in Texas but no wind turbines had been destroyed.

If these systems had been part of microgrids they could have been operable both during and after the storms. But antiquated utility regulations required that they be shut down to prevent power surges that could endanger workers repairing the central grid, even though the technology was now available to isolate the microgrids.

As soon as he found a phone that worked, Branson called Amory Lovins, his partner at the Rocky Mountain Institute. The hurricane set up the perfect experiment for the Institute and a personal challenge for the entrepreneurial billionaire, who set up a fund for introducing innovative energy technology to the stricken islands.

The Caribbean island nations have to pay huge amounts of money to import fossil fuels to power their electric utilities. The cost almost equals the amount they earn from tourism. But if the islands switched to solar and wind energy, which they certainly have in abundance, it would not only cut down on their dependence on fossil fuels, but would make them more resilient and better able to bounce back from future storms.

But Richard Branson wasn't the only billionaire eager to step into the breach left by President Trump's tepid governmental response to history's most costly hurricane.

On October 20 George Page titular head of Google's Project Loon sent hundreds of helium filled balloons from their launching site in Nevada to Puerto Rico. The balloons inflated and deflated, so they could catch winds that would carry them to Puerto Rico then stay stationary over the devastated island.

Working with AT&T and the Federal Communications Agency, Project Loon was able to use the balloons to allow people to start texting with their LTE I-phones thus by-passing 83% of the cell towers that had been destroyed, and helping 3.5 million people start regaining communication with each other and the outside world.

On October 25, Elon Musk, not to be outdone, delivered hundreds of solar panels and energy storing batteries to Hospital del Nino in downtown San Juan near the Contado Beach area know for its high rise hotels, ritzy Cartier and Ferregamo shops and gay nightlife scene.

All of Puerto Rico's hospitals had lost their power and had been operating on generators that emitted nauseating diesel fumes that had not helped those sick and dying. The number of people dying was difficult to determine. Journalists had to start visiting neighborhood morgues to get accurate body counts from the aftermath of the storm and FEMA was no help.

But Musk's vision didn't stop with getting one hospital up and running. The island presented him with the perfect opportunity to test his theory that you could use solar panels and batteries to create microgrids that power people's homes and even their cars, Teslas of course.

Such microgrids would not only be able to stand up better to storms but could be rebuilt and repaired more quickly after the storms passed. These were all important lessons for other hurricane prone coastal areas to learn.

CHAPTER 17
The Pre-Halloween Storm
October 30, 2017

Bushwhacked by the Halloween storm.

The day before Halloween Plum Island was whacked by what New Englanders like to call a wicked bizarre storm. It started as tropical storm Philippe off Cuba. Then Philippe dissipated off Florida and his remains shot north, merging with a deep low-pressure system to become a sub-tropical storm with wind gusts topping 90mph.

It had rained several days before the storm arrived and the trees were still covered with leaves, so hundreds of thousands of them toppled onto roofs, electric wires and across streets. Over 300,000 people were left without power in Massachusetts alone.

Floods floated a house into a bridge in Warren, New Hampshire and schools and businesses were closed throughout the region. They included Governors Academy whose marine biology class had planned to help me measure the storm's erosion on Plum Island.

But I decided to go anyway to take photos. The first thing I noticed as I entered the island were municipal trucks sweeping several inches of sand out of the Center Groin parking lot. It was curious. It didn't look like waves had washed sand over the beach, but that the wind alone had done the deed.

Of greater concern was the river water. It was black. When the North Andover sewage treatment plant lost power, 8 million gallons of raw sewage had flowed into the Merrimack River.

It seemed strange. The plant only had back up generators for their pumping station not for the plant itself.

But interestingly enough, there seemed to be relatively little erosion on Plum Island. Only a few inches had eroded off the dunes in front of the Plum Island Point boardwalk. As I made my way south it was more of the same, less than 5 feet of erosion in front of the houses on Northern Reservation Terrace.

The storm had also blown a lot of sand over the South Jetty but it looked like waves had only washed through the last 70 feet of the ocean end of the structure.

I pondered all this as I walked back to the boardwalk. The tide had gone out just far enough so that I could see that there was more erosion to the north of the boardwalk. I decided to investigate further and discovered that waves on the north side of the wing bar had eroded 10 to 20 feet off the dunes. All that was left were the scarped remains of the high dunes. The beach and low dunes had totally washed away.

Apparently the wingbar separates the beach into two basins a longer one to the south and a shorter one to the north. The wing bar also separates the long period waves into two different wave trains, one that stretches along the entire southern basin so it is less powerful and another that is more focused and powerfully aimed at the north side of the wing bar.

As I drove back to the center of the island, I saw that the wind and waves had also washed most of the sand off the seawalls protecting the houses on Annapolis and Fordham Ways. The beach had disappeared in front of the seawall, leaving its great bulk glistening in the sun that had finally decided to come out.

In the end this strange little storm had been the last storm of the hurricane season that officially finished on November 1. More than that, it was a reminder that the winter erosion season would soon be on us, leaving no time to rebuild the sacrificial dunes in front of Northern Reservation Terrace.

CHAPTER 18
The Lagoon
November 7, 2017

The lagoon snaking across the flats.

On November 7, I finally took the students from Governor's Academy to Plum Island's North Point. It was a cold gray day. Four-foot waves scudded over the choppy waters of the Merrimack River as two Coast Guard cutters returned from a reconnaissance patrol. For months we had been enjoying warm autumn weather, but the recent pre-Halloween storm had finally ushered in more seasonal temperatures.

We measured erosion near the boardwalk and saw where the storm had eroded 20 feet off the dunes toward the end of the point. Then we trudged out to the South Jetty and saw where the storm had jostled the jetty's boulders, causing them to settle another inch or so. One of the gullies that carry sand through the boulders had deepened from about four feet to six feet. All this damage had been caused by repairing the jetty, which had blocked off the natural flow of sand toward North Point.

After the students returned to the academy, I drove to Sandy Point on the southern end of Plum Island. It would allow me to see how the end of a barrier beach island can grow when there are no human structures to interfere with the natural flow of sand.

The first thing I noticed was how difficult it was to walk. Between six and twelve inches of new powdery white sand covered the dunegrass. The Halloween storm had blown sand hundreds of feet into the dunes. It was as if 50 guys with snow blowers had sprayed tons of sand onto the area. It looked like destruction, but the grass would grow up through the sand raising the dunes almost a foot higher the following spring.

The year before, the state had spent almost a month using trucks, Bob Cats and expensive sand imported from a quarry in Maine to build two small sand dunes for $150,000. The night before Halloween, Nature had built up an area four times as large — for free.

There was a lesson here. If you leave a barrier beach alone it will repair itself naturally. It also pointed out that our permitting system is too punitive. It is just as time consuming and expensive to apply for a permit to armor the coast, which should be discouraged, as to spray sand onto the dunes on a regular basis, which should be encouraged. It would be good to have some carrots for good behavior as well as sticks to discourage bad behavior built into the permitting process.

The next thing I noticed was that the last few days of extreme high tides had washed over the spit, and a new six-inch deep inlet was now flowing directly into the center of the lagoon. Just before the Halloween storm, Marc LaCroix and I had flown his drone from Ipswich over Plum Island Sound to photograph the lagoon.

The photographs showed that the spit had finally pinched off the former entrance at the far end of the lagoon. And that the water now flowing over the spit had to go somewhere, so it had scoured out this shallow inlet through the spit into the center of the lagoon.

THE LAGOON

The question was whether sand would seal up the inlet once the so-called king tides, the highest of the year, had passed or whether this new inlet would stay open and migrate over several months, or perhaps even years, to the location of the old inlet a hundred feet away. It all depended on storms and what would happen during the winter, which was fast approaching.

CHAPTER 19
Broken Boulders,
Broken Promises?
November 12, 2017

This boulder in the jetty broke by being jostled in the Halloween storm.

A few days before the MRBA's November meeting I drove to the north end of Plum Island. The mass of Arctic air that had kept us inside had finally moved offshore, leaving just enough autumnal warmth to make it a beautiful windless day.

There was a minus low tide so I could clearly see where the pre-Halloween storm had eroded several feet from beneath the old coast guard station and enough sand out of the cove to reveal the rusty remains of several truck engines that had appeared during the last three winter erosion seasons.

Dead low tide was exactly at noon so I had perfect conditions to see how much sand had also blown over and washed through the jetty during the king tides that had followed.

Sure enough a bright shiny fillet of clean white sand sat on the riverside of the jetty. It was over 200 feet long and perhaps 40 feet wide, about half an acre of sand that was four feet deep.

Waves had already pushed the sand toward the shoreward end of the jetty. In a few days they would push it around the jetty's spur where it would help protect the houses on Northern Reservation Terrace and most intriguing of all, it could provide an inexpensive source of sand to rebuild the sacrificial dunes.

But I found the most hopeful discovery on top of the jetty. Waves from the storm had jostled the jetty so much that one of the multi-ton boulders had cleaved in two, settling the jetty a few more centimeters into the sand. It joined half a dozen other broken boulders that we had been monitoring to gauge how quickly the jetty was settling.

This observation plus the 20 feet of erosion the students from Governor's Academy had measured the week before, showed that the race was on. Either the ocean would undermine the houses of Northern Reservation Terrace this winter or the jetty would settle so enough sand would get through for the beach to start growing again.

Most of all, the situation showed how crucial it was to rebuild the sacrificial dunes so nature would have enough time to return the beach to a state of equilibrium. We would know more about the progress of the project when the Merrimack River Beach Alliance reconvened on November 17.

CHAPTER 20
"The Revenge of the "C" Students."
November 15, 2017

Virginia Institute of Science students core Plum Island's marsh.

Scientists have a snarky term for a phenomenon they call "The Revenge of the "C" Students." It refers to those students closer to the bottom of the class that often end up in regulatory positions where they can decide on the fate of research projects conducted by their brighter classmates. I give myself liberty to use this term since I too was closer to the "C" students.

Unfortunately something akin to "The Revenge of the "C" Students," is hampering our ability to continue living on places like Plum Island. The Marine Biological Laboratory's long-term research project on Plum Island Sound provides a case in point.

It attracts some of the top scientists in the country who have often been the first ones to sound the alarm about the fragility of coastal marshes. But they often have trouble getting permission from state regulators to do small non-invasive pilot projects to understand things like how nutrients flow through a marsh.

Some of these projects have to go through the same permitting process as a developer goes through in order to build a four-story condominium in a marsh.

Researchers with the Massachusetts Bays Program have had similar problems getting permission to cover eight small square meter plots with a thin layer of sand to see whether such sand deposition can counter the effects of sea level rise on marsh grasses.

Shellfish officials have thwarted scientists trying to use blue mussels beds as natural storm surge barriers. Plus, the project to build two sacrificial dunes to protect the houses on Northern Reservation Terrace was delayed by the Natural Heritage Program because of piping plover that nested there 20 years before.

Moreover, it is often difficult for a homeowner to find an engineering firm willing to do a small living shoreline project because the permitting process is just as time-consuming and expensive for a small environmentally sensitive project as for a larger environmentally destructive one. Consequently, far fewer environmentally sensitive projects get done than larger destructive ones.

What we need are as many carrots to encourage environmentally beneficial projects as sticks to discourage destructive ones. This will be the only way we will be able to act proactively to protect the coast rather than to wait until an emergency, when all people can think to do is dump more rocks on the beach.

There were several things that could have been done to protect houses on Plum Island before the 2013 March storm, but they would have had to have been researched and tried five years before the emergency was on us.

By the same token, if we build small sacrificial dunes in front of Northern Reservation Terrace now, we wont be stuck with having to dump ineffectual rocks on the beach under emergency conditions, later. But we wont be able to do innovative projects like these unless the permitting allows for more research and innovation.

There are several ways to streamline the process. One would be to have two tiers of projects, one that would be for more innovative soft engineering research oriented solutions and another for more traditional hard engineering ones.

Another would be to have more of a chain of command, than the present system, which includes several regulatory fiefdoms with their jealously guarded powers and prerogatives. For instance, an agency like the Coastal Zone Management Office, which has responsibility for looking at the big picture, could be the lead agency to usher through beneficial projects instead of having several regulatory agencies that can kill projects on the basis of their own specific concerns.

The MRBA's Senator Tarr had started to revise the permitting process to make it easier for homeowners to protect their homes. Adding carrots to this stew would ensure that we could also incorporate innovative natural solutions so we can live on the coast as long as possible.

CHAPTER 21
Don't Try This at Home
November 21, 2017

*One of the groins that creates a hotspot of erosion
by redirecting longshore currents offshore.*

November 21 was a warm sunny day. I wanted to head to Plum Island, but had had a cold for a week and either the virus or my cough medication had flipped my heart into Atrial Fibrillation.

This happens to me from time to time and usually my heart goes back into normal sinus rhythm after a good night's rest. But the A-fib had already gone on for twenty hours and I was starting to get tired and weak.

I drove myself to the Ipswich clinic where they took an EKG and quickly bundled me into an ambulance bound for Beverly Hospital's Emergency Room. The ambulance seemed excessive. But, note to self, it sure beats waiting for several hours in a busy triage area.

Once I was safely ensconced in my room, I had a front row seat to witness how modern science works at its best. One team of technicians X-rayed my lungs to rule out pneumonia, another took blood to see if I had suffered a stroke. My nurse checked my lungs and found no rhonchi, rales or wheezing and checked my heart and found no murmurs, rubs or gallops. I was particularly happy about that last one.

It was only after eliminating all this extraneous noise that they knew for sure what the problem, or signal, really was. The main problem was to convince my heart to return to its regular heartbeat, and there were two ways to do this.

One was to use electrical paddles to stop my heart so it would restart in normal rhythm; the other was to see if introducing medication into my blood stream would help my heart resolve itself.

Since I had a history of coming out of A-fib on my own, we opted for the medical route. As he introduced the medication into my intravenous line, my nurse explained:

"Now this will take about 10 minutes and I will be checking you after every few drops. We might have to do it several times and you might have to stay overnight. My God you're out!"

A doctor confirmed it, nice regular sinus rhythms.

"So can I go home now? "

I don't know if it is standard procedure but we all gave each other high fives and they prepared me to go home.

The experience gave me time to reflect on how decisions have been made about Plum Island. It would be nice to think that the Army Corps of Engineers uses the scientific method at least as well as nurses in your local ER. Unfortunately they don't. They make political decisions lightly papered over by CYA science.

It would have been like if every organ in my body had a voice in deciding what procedure should be done. Since my coughing was loudest the doctors could have used the squeaky wheel methodology and treated my cough leaving my quiet heart to continue fluttering so ineffectually. In affect they would have solved the wrong problem.

We solved the wrong problem once on Plum Island and are about to do the same thing again. The first time occurred when Newbury residents used local knowledge to bludgeon the Corps of Engineers into repairing the South Jetty when the real problem was the groins, which had created hot spots of erosion in the Annapolis Way area.

Now the cry was to dump hundreds of thousands of tons of sand offshore of Plum Island. But sand was not the problem. Plum Island has plenty of sand accumulated over the past four thousand years. The problem was the repaired jetty that was preventing sand from flowing naturally along the north end of the island to protect the houses of Northern Reservation Terrace.

I'm thankful that the ER doctors didn't rely on my local knowledge, but did their own research to ferret out the real problem. If the Army Corps starts doing real data based science, rather than relying on inaccurate local knowledge, they will probably do a lot fewer projects but start solving a lot more real problems. Doing real science to support innovative solutions to real problems is the only way we can hope to continue living on barrier beach islands in the face of sea level rise.

CHAPTER 22
The Dumbest Development on the East Coast
November 29, 2017

Site of the proposed 204 unit condominium the day after a March storm in 2012.

On November 29, the owners of the largest lot in Salisbury announced plans for the dumbest development on the East Coast.

In the wake of hurricanes that had devastated major cities and flattened island nations, they proposed building a 240 unit, 5-story high condominium complex on one of the most storm ravaged beaches in America.

Calling themselves the Big Block Development Group, the three owners of Salisbury's major nightclubs, lounges and penny arcades had one thing right. The era of honkytonk beachside amusements was over.

But they had the rest wrong. They airily dismissed concerns about flooding, insisting that would all be ironed out in the permitting process. But flooding issues won't just be dealt with in the permitting process.

They will be dealt with in Nature's arena and Nature doesn't like 5 story condominiums on her shores.

Less than five years ago, ocean waves were bursting through the front windows of buildings on this street and firemen pulled the occupants out of the back windows before they drowned in their own living rooms. Earlier storms had swept through this lot depositing sand five blocks inland. A recent study warned that in future storms, Beach Road could be so flooded that Salisbury rescue vehicles would have to drive into New Hampshire then south to reach this part of the island.

So let's look at some of the basic science that the owners ignored. Massachusetts has more major storms than any other state on the East Coast. We haven't had many major hurricanes like Katrina, Sandy, or Maria, in recent years, but that is largely a matter of luck. Despite being so far north we are more than due for such a beach-clearing hurricane.

But we get more than our share of Northeasters and as all New Englanders know, or should know, Northeasters cause the most erosion because they stick around through several tidal cycles.

The developers also displayed their lack of understanding by saying that the building would be elevated above the floodplain so there would be no problem on that score. Wrong again. A major storm along this shore could sweep several tons of sand from beneath such a structure leaving it standing thirty of forty feet out in the Atlantic Ocean to be toppled by the next storm.

Then of course there is the problem of finance. Many local banks have stopped selling mortgages for buildings along this shore. So even if the developers have the cash on hand to build the condominiums, and can flip them before the next major storm, people purchasing the units will have a difficult time purchasing mortgages and be saddled with rapidly rising insurance costs from the Federal Flood Insurance Program that was $24 Billion dollars in debt before this last year of astronomically costly storms.

Besides, who would want to own a condominium in a building that guaranteed to experience several beach clearing storms during the twenty to thirty year lifespan of your mortgage? Can't towns think of more creative ways to raise their tax base than risking the lives and livelihoods of their citizens?

CHAPTER 23
"High Dune"
December 6, 2017

This dune was about 30 feet high, three months later it is only 7 feet high.

December 6 was a warm sunny day with little wind, so I drove to the end of North Point to see the ten-foot high king tide. Long period waves were riding in on top of the wing bar and breaking over the three-foot high berm of sand that protects the dunes.

But the center of this section of the beach was a different story. I walked to the top of the highest dune and stared down at waves that were undermining the toe of the dune thirty feet below. It was a vertiginous experience.

Each wave was tearing away the toe of the bank, creating an avalanche of sand that inched up the vertical face of the sandy cliff. The only thing that was holding the dune together was the matrix of dune grass roots just below my feet.

I gingerly withdrew and continued to where I had first seen a rusty barrel jutting out of the dune several weeks before. Last night's high tide had finally dislodged the barrel and it looked like a pair of city workers had dragged it off the beach. The barrel must have been buried when the Coast Guard built up this dune to slow erosion the last time the south jetty was repaired, in 1969.

But it didn't look good. Two more feet of sand had collapsed off the top of the dune in just the last few days. The back of the dune descended rapidly to a fence that surrounded the Coast Guard's camera tower that allows the Coasties to monitor the bars in the mouth of the river. When such critical federal infrastructure starts to wash away, you can expect to see some action.

Last night's waves had also overtopped the rest of the beach and undermined the remains of the old Coast Guard Station on the other end of the beach. The nearest house was now only 106 feet from the ocean. Unless the state rebuilt the sacrificial dune that slowed erosion so effectively last year, this house and about twenty others would be flooded during the coming winter.

But interestingly enough, it seemed like the reason this end of the beach was not eroding quite as fast as before was that more sand was getting through the jetty. I would have to keep an eye on the situation as the winter progressed.

On December 19 I returned to the high dune to see how much it had eroded during the last ten days. The dune had retreated three more feet, but the dune itself was two feet lower because the top of the dune comes to such a steep crest.

It was sad to see the great dune washing away, but at the same time I felt privileged to witness such rapid change. An alpine geologist would have to wait several thousand years to see this much erosion and if he happened to be looking at the wrong mountain range it could have grown rather than shrunk.

But then I saw something I had never seen before. The base of the cliff had alternate strata of markedly coarse and fine-grained sands. I had see hundreds of examples of such bedding in dunes before, the sand grains might have strikingly different colors but they were always close to the same size. Here the grains were almost an eighth of an inch in one stratum while those in the next were so small I could hardly discern the individual grains.

It turns out the reason I had never seen such bedding is that I had never observed dunes made by rivers before. The Merrimack makes a wide curve just before it enters the Atlantic Ocean. The water travels faster on the wide side of this curve so it carves away sand on the Salisbury side of the river and deposits sand on the Plum Island side where the river's flow is slower.

The deposited sand formed a long wing or point bar that jutted into the river. The strata in these point bars and along the side of the river had been put down by a series of floods and quiet flows. The floods had deposited the large coarse-grained sand while the quiet periods had deposited the finer muds and silts.

So what I had seen was probably the stump of a wing bar that used to jut out from the beach and the same thing is happening today. The danger is that if too much sand clogs the mouth of the river it could cut through Salisbury Beach, leaving the jetties guarding a river that is no longer there.

This was how the river jumped half a mile in the 1800's. Perhaps it was then that this fascinating bedding was first deposited along this short stretch of beach.

CHAPTER 24
The Hunter
December 9, 2017

Hunter rounds the dune on Sandy Point.

December 9 was another cold gray day. It was supposed to start snowing at 10:00am so I wanted to get to southern end of Plum Island early. It might be the last time I could see the Sandy Point lagoon because the Parker River Wildlife Refuge closes the lower road as soon as the snow flies, and sometimes doesn't reopen it until Spring.

I was surprised how many photographers were out at 9:00am on such a cold day. Each of the seven parking lots had half a dozen cars and scrums of photographers were encamped on the side of the road, searching for snowy owls.

There is an ongoing debate about how much photographers disrupt the owls, which have come this far south because of lack of food on the Arctic Tundra. The young owls have never seen humans before, particularly large packs of humans seemingly intent on dislodging the owls from their feeding territories that already provide little enough protein for the magnificent birds. What photographers often think are cute behaviors like yawning or staring into the camera lens are usually signs of distressed birds trying to defend their home turf.

What is not controversial is how much these modern day hunters spend on the tripods, lenses and the new digital cameras that have opened up the field to so many new participants. They represent a new use of our national wildlife refuge system that adds economic value to the surrounding communities.

The south end of the island was largely the same when I was out here a month before. But the sandbar that made up the southern side of the lagoon had grown higher and longer, setting up an interesting scenario. As the sandbar grew it had curved back to the north, pinching off the opening to the lagoon between the sandbar and a six -foot high sanddune on the island.

Water rushing in and out of the lagoon had eroded several feet off the dune, but the sandbar had grown two feet higher and twenty feet longer, so Sandy Point was both growing and eroding, but the growth was of a low sandbar and the erosion was from a six foot high dune. It also didn't help that people liked to climb the twenty-foot high dune that overlooked the hundred foot long lagoon.

"Blam! Blam!" My reveries were interrupted by the sound of a nearby shotgun. I knew the Refuge's one-day deer hunt had been a few days before. So what was this? A few minutes later the perpetrator came sauntering down the beach with shotgun and portable blind in hand. A little further down the beach I spotted where a diving duck had been killed and eviscerated probably by a snowy owl or a peregrine falcon that dive on their prey from above at 200 miles per hour.

The next day I posted a photograph of the hunter on the Refuge's photography site and all hell broke lose. Most of the photographers weren't aware that duck hunting was allowed on the landward side of the Refuge and along the shores of Sandy Point state park on the south end of the island. In fact it was revenue from the sale of duck stamps that hunters had to buy with their licenses that mostly supported the federal system of wildlife refuges.

Allowing hunting on the landward side of the refuge represented an interesting compromise. Before the Refuge was established, people hunted ducks on both sides of Plum Island Sound and the fusillade of sounds and lead drove ducks offshore where they couldn't dive for food.

When the Refuge closed the Plum Island side, hunters scared the ducks out of the landward marshes but the ducks quickly learned that nobody would shoot them on the island side of the Refuge, where they could find more than enough food to fuel their migrations south. Some ducks and geese even found the Refuge so congenial they started to spend the winter along with snowy owls, those iconic environmental refugees of our ever-warming planet.

CHAPTER 25
The French Connection
December 12, 2017

On December 12, exactly the two years after 198 nations agreed on the Paris Climate Accords, French President Emanuel Macron announced the first winners of his "Make Our planet Great Again" project.

When I first read about the proposal I thought it was just a publicity stunt tweaking President Trump for his "Make America Great Again" slogan. After all the grants would be for the duration of President Trump's term in office.

But as I looked more closely I realized that his initiative represented a real brain drain threatening American leadership on climate change research, which is arguably the most important problem facing our nation today.

In all eighteen hundred top climate scientists applied for the grants including eleven hundred from the United States. The first 18 winners were senior scientists from institutions like Princeton, Stanford and Cornell. Five were government scientists from the National Center for Atmospheric Research and the National Renewable Energy Laboratory in Colorado.

Fifty scientists in all would receive their moving expenses to France and between 1 million and 1.5 million Euros, $118,000 to $1.76 million, to pursue their research interests.

The United States had spent several hundred thousand dollars each training these scientists and their loss will reverberate through the climate science field for decades after Trump has exited the White House.

It would be yet another consequence of Trump's rash decision to pull out of the 2015 Climate Accords ceding leadership to Europe, China and Russia and leaving places like Plum Island without the research it needs to survive in a world of inexorably rising seas.

CHAPTER 26
The Bill
December 16, 2017

Some poor sod (Eric Fisher) standing in the cold
explaining which house will tumble into the ocean next.

Anyone who has spent very much time in Massachusetts knows exactly where all her hotspots of erosion are located.

If a hurricane is approaching from the South you will see some poor weatherperson standing in the rain forecasting exactly where to expect flooding on Martha's Vineyard, Nantucket and the south shore of Cape Cod.

If a Northeaster is threatening you will see the same poor sod standing in the snow explaining exactly which houses will tumble into the ocean in Scituate, Marshfield and on Plum Island.

You are less likely to hear how each separate community deals with problems after the storms have passed. Chatham might hire a Woods Hole scientist to elucidate how to deal with her three inlets that open and close over a 140-year cycle.

Newbury will probably look the other way as homeowners build illegal seawalls to provide them with a false sense of security. Salisbury developers will propose building a five story high condominium on a beach that could retreat two hundred feet over the 20-year life of the owners' mortgages.

At the same time, beach owners like the Cape Cod National Seashore, the Parker River Wildlife Refuge, the Trustees of Reservations and town like Orleans will face facts and move buildings and parking lots landward in the face of the ever-rising Atlantic Ocean.

But now there is a bill before the Massachusetts Legislature, which would create a process to deal with erosion in a coordinated manner throughout the state.

With 1500 miles of shoreline, Massachusetts has the 4th longest coast of any other state on the East Coast. Why even my hometown, Orleans, has twice as much coast as the entire state of New Hampshire.

The bill before the legislature would make all the approaches by separate towns part of a coordinated effort to protect the commonwealth's shorelines. Called the Comprehensive Adaptation Management Plan, the bill would create an interagency advisory committee, lightly modeled on The Merrimack River Beach Alliance. The interagency committee would consider strategies based on a set of best management practices.

The committee would then promote research on the vulnerability of communities to climate change and provide grants to assist cities and towns in combating their flooding and erosion problems. Most importantly it would also establish a program to buy back properties threatened by erosion and convert the empty lots into public conservation areas.

The bill had passed the Senate and was now before the House Ways and Means Committee. If it passed it would expand on Governor Charley Baker's 2016 executive order for a plan to deal with climate change and codify it into perhaps the most forward thinking erosion policy in the United States. A policy that would hopefully help grease the wheels to rebuild the Northern Reservation Terrace sacrificial dune system that had been dead in the water since last spring.

CHAPTER 27
Approaching Equilibrium
December 29, 2017

About as much sand was filling in the cove as was eroding off the dunes, approaching a state of equilibrium.

December 29 was a bitterly cold day with wind chills in the negative digits. Rime ice clung to the exposed roots of dune grass dangling from the steeply scarped dunes north of the boardwalk.

The dunes' jagged profile had changed so radically during just the last ten days of erosion that it took me awhile to figure out where I had measured from before. As erosion had swept inland it had lopped ten feet off the peak of some dunes, while others appeared to have grown 5 feet because as the erosion advanced it had exposed some of the higher dunes. But now there was only a single line of dunes left before the ocean would reach the fence surrounding the Coast Guard's property and the wellhead of the state's depuration plant built to cleanse clams dug from polluted flats.

After taking my measurements I rushed back to make the 10:30am meeting of the Merrimack River Beach Alliance. But it was a deeply frustrating meeting. Everyone seemed to be repeating what had already been said before about getting permits to receive material dredged from the Piscataqua River in Maine. However the dredging had yet to be funded and was scheduled to start in 2019 at the earliest.

Meanwhile the winter erosion season was already half over and nothing had been done about rebuilding the dunes in front of the houses on Northern Reservation Terrace. Finally I couldn't stand it any longer and gave my figures for the 60 feet of erosion we had recorded since October in the dunes north of the boardwalk and the relative lack of severe erosion on the portion of the beach in front of Northern Reservation Terrace.

I even presented my hunch that so much sand was now blowing over or washing through the jetty that the beach had started to grow at the same time the dunes above it were eroding. This meant that the houses on Northern Reservation Terrace could still be flooded this winter, but that the beach itself was growing so fast that the houses would be considerably safer by next winter.

I was uncomfortable going so far out on a limb. A scientist would never do so when his hunch was still just a thought experiment. But, as a writer, I felt it was important that people had the information, even though it was so preliminary.

After the meeting I asked Bruce Tarr and his new legislative assistant if I could join them as they inspected the beach. I was quite sure Senator Tarr's aide never thought he would be trudging down the beach in minus degree weather rather than lounging around the nice warm rotunda of the State House lobby. We joshed Mike that he should have selected a more sedentary senator and for gosh sakes to bring a warmer coat to any future meetings. But it was just too damn cold to wait another hour for low tide.

So the next day I returned at dead low tide in order to measure the buildup of sand along the spur of the jetty. Sure enough, the boulders were already being buried under 4 feet of sand, the cove landward of the spur was filling in, and the slope of the beach in front of Northern Reservation was now long and gradual. This would provide a longer run up so waves wouldn't break directly on the dune face during moderate weather, but could slide over the dunes.

These measurements all pointed to the fact that the Northern Reservation Terrace houses could be safer next winter, but they also made it even more imperative that the sacrificial dune be rebuilt, so there would be something left to save the following winter.

CHAPTER 28
The Bomb Cyclone
January 4, 2018

The bomb cyclone' hits the North Shore. Shari Melto photo.

During the last days of December and the first days of January, New England struggled through ten days of unrelenting cold. Then, on January 4 things got even worse.

Winter storm Grayson had started as a low-pressure storm off the coast of Florida that dumped snow and ice in peculiar places unused to such weather. So many iguanas fell out of ice-rimmed trees that officials warned people not to touch the foot long creatures, who had a chance to survive if they were not handled.

The average temperature of the entire United States was calculated to be nine degrees Fahrenheit, making our planet colder than Mars. Then Grayson swirled into another storm that had been spawned in the Pacific. The combined cyclone then bombed, dropping its central pressure 53 millimeters in 24 hours. This matched the barometric pressure reached by Hurricane Sandy just before it landed its left hook on New Jersey.

Every storm has a characteristic that catches forecasters off guard. For Hurricane Sandy it was the surprise left hook, for our pre-Halloween storm it was the number of fallen trees that left hundreds of thousands of people without power. It was the tides with this storm. They were actually an extension of the king tides that had peaked in November but had continued to pass through the tide charts like a pig in a python reading 10.1 feet for Plum Island on January 4.

It was the storm surge riding on top of these tides that took motorists by surprise. People who had been driving through a few inches of water as high tide peaked were suddenly engulfed by three extra feet of water as the storm surge overtook them.

Dozens of cars were swamped near the Boston Aquarium as a five-block area was covered with four feet of seawater, much of the water cascading down the steps of the nearby subway station in a scene reminiscent of New York during Hurricane Sandy.

The same thing happened in community after community as high tide approached. People had to be rescued out of cars in Boston, Scituate and Marshfield, and thirty-two cars were flooded in Chelsea. Gloucester officials had directed people to park in the high school parking lot so the city's streets could be plowed only to find that the storm filled 60 of the cars with standing water.

Reporters for WBUR were flooded when waves swept down the street in Scituate right after they had covered the rescue of the town's harbormaster who had fallen into the water while attempting to secure a boat line. And in Rockport, waves hurled rocks the size of grapefruit over houses along the battered Atlantic shore.

Similar things happened on Plum Island. The storm surge unexpectedly attacked the island from the Plum Island Sound side, closing the only access point to the island and inundating the low-lying Plum Bush downs area. Sewer lines broke and propane tanks floated free.

The floods set off a fire alarm in Shari Melto's house and the water was so deep firefighters had to be carried to her house in the shovel of a high water rescue vehicle.

Five Plum Island families sought shelter in PITA Hall while police scanners in the newsroom of the Daily News crackled with calls from people who had failed to heed warnings to evacuate the island as 13 foot waves pounded her shores from Northern Reservation Terrace to the lagoon on Sandy Point.

But the storm was only the beginning. Over a foot of snow and ocean water froze on Plum Island Turnpike, as what the Washington Post's weather editor called "wicked cold air sourced from Siberia, the North Pole and Greenland plunged the wind chill to minus 24 degrees." Now there was a displaced New Englander for sure.

Chapter 29
The Perfect Storm?
January 7, 2018

Mystery pipe revealed by the Bomb Cyclone Storm.

On January 7, I drove to Plum Island to measure the erosion from the Bomb Cyclone storm. It was the first day that the dead low tide would fall at a reasonable enough daylight hour so I could see how much sand had buried the spur of the jetty.

The spur acts like an attached breakwater, and during the storm it had encouraged about a hundred feet of sand to grow out from the beach and about 50 feet of sand to grow landward from the spur into the rapidly filling cove behind the spur.

This meant that at the same time that the dunes had eroded 10 to 15 feet, the beach in front of them had grown over a hundred feet, developing a smooth gentle slope that would help absorb the energy of future storms.

Even more encouraging was the sandbar inside the jetty. More than two acres of sand holding at least 20,000 cubic yards of sediment had washed through the jetty. It was too frigid to clamber over the jetty to measure how much of the sandbar consisted of sand and how much was ice jammed up against the new bar. So it was difficult to get an exact figure.

But a few days later it was warm enough to see what had happened. The sand held back by the jetty looked like a scoured riverbed. The ten foot tide and 13 foot waves had created a ridge and runnel system, making a river that had coursed down the beach and cut through 5 feet of sand that it had then washed through the jetty.

A hole six feet long, four feet wide and several feet deep formed a sluiceway where the water had rushed through. But the sluiceway was right beside a boulder that had broken in two during a previous storm and it showed that the jetty was starting to break apart the way it had during the Blizzard of 1978. Further evidence lay in the sand below the jetty. Several one ton boulders were lying in the Merrimack River after they had tumbled off the jetty during the storm.

Weather forecasters made a big deal that the tides from the Bomb Cyclone storm had beat the high tide records set by the 1978 Blizzard, but that wasn't really accurate. The Bomb Cyclone tides had been about the same or even lower than in 1978, but the sea level had risen 5 inches since 1978, so it looked like our recent tide was higher.
And according to Bruun's Rule, an esoteric rule of thumb used by coastal geologists, every 5 inches of sea level rise will translate into between 40 and 166 feet of coastal retreat. Of course, Northern Reservation Terrace was already retreating 150 feet every winter!

But now that the jetty was disheveling things were looking better. If I had been asked to give odds before the storm on the chances that the houses on Northern Reservation Terrace would be flooded during the winter, I would have said close to 100 percent. But now the chances were about 50 percent, and if sand kept washing through the disheveled jetty, the odds could drop to close to zero by next year. Good news for the homeowners.

One of the homeowners was Vern Ellis who invited me and a fellow photographer into his Northern Reservation Terrace home to warm up from the wind and cold. It provided enough respite so we could continue to measure how the north end of the beach had fared.

As I walked out to the end of the boardwalk and looked right, it was encouraging. The beach had a huge new bulge of sand that had washed there from both the north and south. But the boardwalk itself was alarming. The overwash had lapped the ramp leading to the gazebo and torn another few feet off the adjoining duneface.

But looking to the north was truly alarming. The first thing I saw was a large pipe protruding about nine feet out of the dune. It was thirteen inches in diameter and looked like some kind of outfall pipe — but an outfall pipe to what?

It didn't make sense that the pipe would be from the depuration wellhead, because it was sticking out perpendicularly from the beach. Was it perhaps a drainpipe from the nearby parking lot, or perhaps a discharge pipe from a former Coast Guard building? It was a mystery but a few days later you could see that the pipe lined up with the public restrooms. Hopefully the pipe was no longer being used!

But it was the dunes that were most alarming. They had retreated more than ten feet during the storm. The measuring stake that had been fourteen and a half feet from the edge of the highest dune before the storm was now only a foot and a half away. The dune itself was almost ten feet lower and would lose another five feet as the dune sought its angle of repose.

In all, these dunes had retreated 20 feet in October, 24 feet in November, 27 feet in December and 13 feet during just the first week of January. Plus, there was now a potential new breakthrough area where the ocean could rush through the low dunes.

We could expect another 70 feet of erosion in the next three months and still nothing had been done to rebuild the sacrificial dune to protect the houses on Northern Reservation Terrace.

But the storm had been somewhat of an anomaly. It had been strong enough to dishevel the jetty but not strong enough to damage the houses on Northern Reservation Terrace. Had it been the perfect storm? We would have to see.

CHAPTER 30
Same Problem, Different Island
Turks and Caicos
January 15, 2018

Groin blocking the flow of sand down the beach.

Right after the Bomb Cyclone Storm, I flew to the Turks and Caicos Islands for a much-anticipated vacation with my sister and her husband. My sister is one of those fortunate people who has been befriended by a wild dolphin, who breaks the mold set by animal behaviorists. JoJo dives everyday with my sister, has deliberately introduced her to two generations of dolphins and regularly plays jokes like nudging nurse sharks towards groups of tourists diving on the reefs to make them freak out and streak toward the surface.

But the most interesting thing that JoJo has done has been to create a new culture, a group of dolphins that seek out human companionship plus a culture in which male dolphins babysit for infants while their mothers go off fishing.

My secondary reason for visiting Turks and Caicos was to see how the largest island, Providenciales, had fared during Hurricane Irma. The island had certainly taken a hard hit. Many areas had been severely damaged but nobody had been killed. The island seemed to have done everything right, shutting off electricity to the entire island before the storm and pre-delivering sheetrock and lumber so recovery could immediately begin after the storm.

Nature also helped. It rained after Irma and places that had been stripped of all vegetation started sprouting new shoots only days later. Now the entire island was covered with four feet of lush green native underbrush, hiding the stumps of the snapped off Casuarina and Palm Trees that had been imported from Australia and Florida.

But the real story was how little damage had occurred on some parts of the island. The winds had battered the north side of the island, but the south coast, where many of the resorts were built only ten feet above sea level, had survived. Part of the reason lay in the topography of the coast. If you visit the small islands immediately to the north of Providenciales you can see outcrops of tumbled down limestone that have eroded twenty feet in the past twenty years.

But almost no erosion had occurred along the fifteen miles of gently curving beach that encompasses the aptly named Grace Bay. It is one of the most beautiful beaches in the world, but it also encircles a huge basin of tiny white spheres of ootolite sand. The sand is composed of the small bits of limestone that have washed off the outcrops and been covered with concretions of calcium carbonate from the seawater to make the perfectly rounded grains.

The curvature of the bay holds in this huge basin of sand that sloshes back and forth absorbing the energy of storm surges and waves from battering the coast itself. When the basin of sand gets to be about ten miles deep it will start to lithify into sandstone because of the heat and pressure of the overlying sand. Plate tectonics will eventually push the sandstone to the surface in the form of mountains and volcanoes, but the individual sand grains will be on their own endless voyage and survive, achieving an immortality of sorts.

It is this constant churning of the geology of the earth that makes the biology of our planet possible. It is strange that humans think they can build houses on the edge of this churning and think they will survive for the 80 year span of their lives or even the 20 year span of the artificially determined mortgages on their homes.

Toward the evening we were invited to an impromptu dinner by the crew members of two yachts visiting the island, from Italy and Mexico. The Italian yacht had already put on its underwater lights that silhouetted us against this turquoise blue background. The lights also attracted myriads of tiny plankton that darted in and out of the bright lights. The plankton had in turn attracted swimming crabs that held pieces of sargassum below their bodies to hide from the schools of jack attracted to the movable feast.

But the crew members attention was directed toward schools of four to five foot tarpon lurking in the shadows beyond the pale of light. Every so often a tarpon would lunge to the surface and open its foot-long squarish mouth to suck in one of the hapless crabs.

Some of the crew members were using the crabs for bait to hook the tarpon, which stood on their tails and leapt into the air before they were released back into the channel to the applause of and delight of the rest of the crew members.

The scene was the perfect example of the diversity and abundance of organisms created by the interaction of the geology and biology of our fortunate planet.

CHAPTER 31
Snatching Defeat from the Jaws of Victory?
January 26, 2018

The cove was filling in so rapidly it could become a
new source of sand for a sacrificial dune system.

Northern Reservation Terrace was awash with rumors before the January meeting of the Merrimack River Beach Alliance. First, residents had heard that rebuilding the sacrificial dune would be on the agenda, and then they heard it had been taken off.

So I was relieved when I drove up to PITA Hall and saw that the parking lot was full. For the first time since the spring, administrators from both the Massachusetts Department of Conservation and Recreation, that owns North Point Beach, and Newburyport, that manages it, would be sitting at the same table.

The meeting started off with the usual exhortations that time was running short and that if Newbury, Newburyport and Salisbury wanted to join with Hull and Scituate to apply for 680,000 cubic yards of Piscataqua River sand, they had to apply to a new pilot program before March 9.

A working group was appointed, consisting of officials from the three North Shore communities and lead by Newbury because they had signed up first. The working group's initial job would be to select a consultant to do the permitting work. That would be easy because the environmental firm GZA had done such a good job building the first dual dune system.

Finally the meeting arrived at what everybody had come for, what to do about protecting Northern Reservation Terrace. Mike Driscoll, the head of the DCR's Waterways Division launched into a long peroration about all the important work that the division was doing to transect and model the shores of every coastal community in the Commonwealth. But the mayor of Newburyport, Donna Holladay, voiced the frustration of everyone in the room, pointedly declaring, "We are drowning in studies. Meanwhile North Point is eroding more than twenty feet every two weeks."

Under pressure, Driscoll admitted that DCR had no money immediately budgeted for such work but that they could probably rebuild the dune with sand scheduled to be dredged from beneath George Charos' dock in March. After doing such an excellent job the year before, had the DCR just snatched defeat from the jaws of victory? Would they be a day late and a dollar short?

The beach in front of Northern Reservation Terrace was growing so fast that a sacrificial dune would probably not be needed by the spring. But it would be crucially needed for the storms that arrived every other week on average in February and March.

And now there was a new source of sand. The last time I wrote about the cove that lies landward of the spur of the jetty it had been in October and I had talked about being able to dredge sand from the bottom of the shallow cove. But since October, the cove had filled with six more feet of new sand. That was enough to fill two football fields worth of sand six feet deep, and it was now completely exposed at low tide.

This meant that instead of a dredge, a bulldozer could be used to safely skim one to two feet off the surface of the exposed sand, between 3,000 and 4,000 cubic yards, and push it up against the existing dune. Even if all the sand were washed away the project would still be a success because it would have absorbed the energy of the storms, thus protecting the original natural dunes.

When the sand washed off the dunes it would just wash back into the cove that was filling in so rapidly that the spur of the jetty would be fully buried under six feet of sand by the summer. Of course the project might raise red flags because it would be so simple. Permitting agencies are more effective dealing with larger more expensive projects.

The meeting ended with discussions of two ways to fund such projects. Senator Kathleen O'Connor Ives outlined a plan to create a trust fund from revenue generated by the North Point parking lot and Vern Ellis announced that residents of Northern Reservation Terrace would hold a series of fund raising events in the summer.

But if Nature had her way, and she always does, further sand might not be necessary. Northern Reservation Terrace could make it through the winter with only damage caused by overwash.

CHAPTER 32
The Stealth Missile
February 1, 2018

*A solid wall of homes built on the same footprint
as the houses that had fallen into the ocean in 2012.*

On February 1, the town of Newbury signed a contract with the Army Corps of Engineers for a Section 103 study. This meant they had beat other communities from applying and guaranteed that they would be the lead agency for a new pilot project to use additional federal funds to dump dredged sand off the beach.

Doug Packer, Newbury's Conservation Agent, had negotiated the contract to study a 2,000 linear foot stretch of beach from Central Groin south, to develop a plan and build a berm that could protect that shoreline's oceanfront homes.

It seemed a bit unfair on the face of it. At the behest of their lobbyist, Newbury homeowners had convinced the Corps to put 250 Newburyport homes at risk by repairing the Merrimack River jetties. Didn't their mothers teach them to pick up after themselves before moving on to the next project? By all rights the Corps should have been building a berm in front of the houses on Northern Reservation Terrace to make up for their $24 Million dollar mistake.

But you had to hand it to Newbury for applying before their neighbors. Since Newburyport didn't own the beach in front of Northern Reservation Terrace, the real owners, the Massachusetts Department of Conservation and Recreation would have had to apply. But they had other things on their minds, like the rest of the Commonwealth's 1500 miles of shoreline.

The contract required Newbury to contribute $195,000 to do the study, plus 35% of construction costs, and more money if the Corps determined it was necessary.

The specifics seemed to have come about because of Newbury's dis-satisfaction with a Woods Hole study that popped the long held belief that sand flows south along Plum Island's entire shoreline. The Woods Hole scientists showed that sand erodes off Newbury, the center of the island, then flows in two distinct sand cells; one from the center of the island north to Newburyport, and the other another from the center of the island south to Sandy Point.

The implications of the Woods Hole study were plain to see. There was not a whole lot you could do to stop erosion in the Newbury section of the island, but there were several things you could do to help the ends of the island continue to grow naturally.

In a perfect world decision makers would have taken this information and planned a prudent course of action. For instance they might have discouraged people from rebuilding on lots whose houses had washed away in storms like the one in 2012.

If those lots had been left empty it would have increased the land values and revenue from the homes behind them. In some instances the owners of the second tier homes also owned the first tier homes. But apparently they wanted to squeeze as much money as possible from their oceanfront investments.

But Newbury's actions turned what could have been a prudent course of action into a purely political process. If the Merrimack Valley Regional Planning board could hire the Woods Hole Group, then Newbury could have their own experts. Who better to hire than the most "can do" of all government agencies, the pork barrel fed Army Corps of Engineers?

But there were some glimmers of hope. The contract stated that in addition to developing places for berms and dunes, "It was expected that at least one additional reasonable alternative would be identified during the feasibility study".

It was interesting that the contract specified that the study would concentrate on the 2,000 linear of shoreline that stretches south from the Plum Island Turnpike. That stretch also encompassed groins that redirected sand offshore both during storms and during the intervening calm periods. So that at present, there was no beach on which to build berms because waves reflecting off the seawalls had washed the beaches offshore.

If the groins were to be removed or reworked into breakwaters the beach would grow back naturally to about sixty feet during high tides and a hundred feet during low tides. Then you would have a platform to build berms on.

But unless and until Plum Island got rid of its groins no solution, whether it be dunes or sand dumped offshore, would last for more than a few short years. But perhaps it didn't really matter; sand from those structures would flow north onto Newburyport's beaches anyway.

CHAPTER 33
Tsunami Alert
February 6, 2018

After a 700 foot stretch of waves pass through the jetties they spread out into a 1400 foot stretch of waves that are about half as high and half as powerful.

At 8:30 in the morning on February 6 thousands of people from Portland Maine to Houston, Texas received a shock when they turned on their phones. There was a severe weather alert for a tsunami aimed at their specific county.

It didn't take long for the National Weather Service to fess up. The alert had been part of a monthly test that somehow had been picked up and broadcast through AccuWeather's mobile phone app. The Internet was immediately flooded with people joking they had survived the tsunami on Plum Island, Cape Hatteras or Galveston Texas.

But the incident reminded me of a symposium I had attended in Woods Hole about the Fukushima tsunami. It was one of those wonderful Woods Hole seminars whose panel included young researchers who had just returned from the site as well as wise old scientists who had spent their entire careers studying such problems.

Heather Goldstone was the moderator of the symposium. She was also something of a local hero. Immediately after receiving her PhD from the joint Woods Hole MIT Oceanography program she had walked up the street of the small coastal village and knocked on the door of a local radio station housed in a former Xerox office. Her offer was to do science stories for the nascent public radio station. It was the perfect gig for a newly minted science writer. Every day this tiny coastal village generated more science stories than most major cities. Soon she had her own show and had picked up a national following.

Heather closed the symposium with a question one of her former professors used to ask visiting scientists, "If your reputation was not a consideration, what problem would you feel is un-fundable but critical to the future?"

A senior scientist answered right away. He would like to research the possibility of a 150-foot tsunami enveloping the East Coast. And there was a candidate to trigger such an event. The flank of the Cumbre Viejo Volcano in the Canary Islands was poised to collapse and plunge into the Atlantic Ocean.

If the 500 cubic kilometer chunk of the mountain collapsed all at once it would raise a 2000-foot high tsunami that would race across the Atlantic at the speed of a jumbo jet and still be 150 tall when it smashed into the East Coast.

The big question was whether the flank of the mountain would collapse all at once or episodically over several weeks. Either way it gives you great pause when a well-respected scientist tells you what keeps him up all night.

What had been keeping me up all night was trying to visualize why waves had eroded Plum Island's northern high dunes so quickly, and the tsunami alert provided me with just the prod I needed to look into the matter in more detail.

When I first started looking at the mouth of the Merrimack River I was perplexed. It didn't seem to matter how high the waves were offshore or what direction they were coming from. They were almost the same size when they broke on the high dunes as they had been when they were at sea. How could that be?

For instance, the north jetty effectively blocks large waves from northeasters from entering the mouth of the river, yet waves almost that tall seemed to regenerate inside the mouth then slam into the high dunes.

Eventually I did some research and discovered that when waves pass through an aperture they spread out into longer waves with less energy.

In the case of Plum Island, the aperture is the 720-foot opening between the two jetties. So when a 700-foot stretch of waves passes through the jetties, it spreads out to almost 1400 foot long curved waves that are about half as high and contain about half as much energy as the offshore waves.

But when the 700-foot stretch of waves encounters the wingbar, the shallow waters slow the waves down and focus their energy, so they grow back to almost the same height and hold almost as much energy as they did offshore.

It was all this focused energy that tore away 74 feet of the high dune almost as effectively in a month as what a tsunami would have done in just a few minutes.

CHAPTER 34
The Sluiceway
February 7, 2018

*This hole was 6 feet long and 4 feet wide so that
a duck used it to swim through the jetty.*

My stated reason for going to the beach every week is to measure the changes wrought by erosion, but my real reason is to be moved by the power of nature in this incredible universe we inhabit.

Sometimes these experiences were illustrative of larger forces. Sometimes they are just plain amusing. A few days after the bomb cyclone storm a friend of mine was taking photographs of the deep hole the storm had created in the sand above the jetty. As she was shooting a panorama of the scene she heard a quack at her feet.

"Now how the hell did you get there, duck?"

The duck ruffled his feathers, plunged down through the hole, swam through the jetty and popped up in the Merrimack River twenty feet downstream.

Three weeks later the hole was excavated a few feet deeper with the aid of a once in a lifetime display of celestial exuberance. As if to celebrate the end of 31 days of freezing cold, bomb genesis storms, broken down cars, flu and unrelenting erosion, the damnable month of January finally rewarded us.

The January 31st full moon was so large it looked like we were on another planet. This was not an, illusion the moon really was 30,000 miles closer to the earth than usual. It was also a blue moon, the second full moon in the month, a rare occurrence that gives rise to the expression once in a blue moon.

Then the shadow of the earth crossed over the face of the moon, turning it blood red from the reflected light of the earth's recent sunrise. At this moment, priests in ancient Mexico would have happily ripped out the beating hearts of a thousand warriors to bring back the sun. Our Bible prophesied that the sun will turn black, a solar eclipse; and then the moon would turn blood red, a lunar eclipse, before the end of times.

Of course we now live in a more civilized era and know that the blood red lunar eclipse just altered the universe enough to make the Patriots lose the Super Bowl.

It was in this dismal frame of mind that I decided to return to the jetty to seek solace from nature. February 7 seemed like the first feasible day to do so. Five inches of snow followed by two inches of rain were due to fall but the snow wasn't supposed to start until 11:00am and dead low tide was at 10:51am. I figured I had just enough time to make my measurements before it started snowing in earnest.

Even though it was an overcast day with the taste of snow in the air, it was calm and the temperature was in the comfortable thirties. So it was a pleasant walk.

Several of the holes above the jetty had partially filled in, leaving steep sided pits lined with sliding sand. I walked gingerly around the pits hoping the claw of a giant ant lion wouldn't shoot out and drag me under, like in the movie *Dune*.

I finally decided to stop such ruminations and measure the depth of one of the holes that was still open. It reached down 5 vertical feet before it tunneled 15 feet through the jetty to the river. This was significant because it meant the sluiceway was as deep, if not deeper than the original jetty. So sand could flow freely through the jetty at high tide.

It also meant that the holes presented some danger. A child, small pet or even an adult could tumble into one of the holes filled with swiftly flowing water. During storms, water would even explode up through the sand creating new holes.

It would make sense for the city to send someone out with a Bob Cat to fill in the cavities. While they were at it they might even push a little extra sand into the holes since they were another source of local sand that could be used to grow the beach in front of Northern Reservation Terrace.

On the lower beach, several 5 foot long chunks of the old coast guard station's parking lot had tumbled onto the sand and several more would probably do so on the next high tide.

Waves were also tearing away clumps of dunegrass from off the second sacrificial dune and the wrackline was now only 50 feet from the nearest home. And there had still been no action taken to repair the sacrificial dunes.

Finally I reached what I had been calling the high dunes at the end of North Point, but they were no longer so high. Only a month before the highest dune towered 30 feet above the beach.

Now the highest dune was less than twelve feet and the wellhead for the plant that the state used to cleanse shellfish and for research was in a low spot only twelve feet from the rapidly encroaching ocean.

When the ocean reached the wellhead, managers would have to start pumping water out of the Merrimack River, which had already experienced several discharges of raw sewerage in just the past few months.

But by eleven thirty it had started to snow in earnest so I jumped into my car, just in time to get stuck behind a mile long traffic jam of hundreds of students that had been let go early because of the storm. It was pretty impressive; the weather forecasters had predicted the timing of the snow right on the nose!

CHAPTER 35
A Bittersweet Day
February 15, 2018

This multi-ton boulder was frozen in ice and bumped and scrapped 15 feet along the shore. Note the band of clean granite where the boulder used to be buried under the sediments.

February 15 was warm and balmy, the first day of the year that temperatures slipped comfortably above fifty degrees. I decided it would be the perfect day to search for harbingers of spring. I seemed like a good plan. Spring birds were already singing their courtship songs and red-winged blackbird males had begun to establish nesting territories in the swale of phragmites beside our house.

The catkins of weeping willows were glistening yellow in the mid-day sun and the field was covered with standing water from recent rainstorms. It would not be long before the nighttime temperatures would rise above forty degrees and thousands of spring peepers would flock into vernal ponds to mate and lay their eggs. Roman orgies had nothing on what you can see on a cool spring night in a vernal pond.

But when I walked down through the shaded path that led to the marsh I was plunged back into winter. The path was covered with a slippery slope of snow and ice.

I had gone out specifically to see pussy willows but was sadly disappointed. They were still just tiny brown scales on the smooth gray branches of the trees. It would take several more weeks of sunshine for them to fully blossom.

But as I approached the marsh something entirely different caught my attention. It looked like a giant steaming coprolite just deposited by a passing dinosaur. But there were no dinosaurs about and the dung was surrounded with a twenty-foot circle of shells and gray mud.

I realized the coprolite was really just a large chunk of marsh that had frozen to the bottom of a foot thick slab of floating ice that had grounded and melted on this spot. If the ice had floated over the marsh its curious load of mud and detritus would have killed off the underlying marsh grass. This would have created a depression just deep enough to hold rainwater, which would kill off any marsh grass rhizomes intent on colonizing the new area. The fresh water could slowly eat down through the marsh like tooth decay until it had created a several foot deep panne of weed filled water, a boon for ducks but doom for any horse or human who happened to get stuck in the pannes' mud filled bottoms. On the other hand, the storm had added 10 years worth of sediment to the marsh.

But there was another more subtle sign of spring where the high tide had covered the causeway. There was a ten-foot long stretch of inky black anaerobic mud just beneath the shallow water. But now the weak sun was already encouraging blue-green algae and zinc white bacteria to slowly cover the mud that had been below the ice with mats of green purple and white filaments. In the summer the algae would be festooned with silvery bubbles of pure oxygen. This is what life looked like for millions of years as blue-green algae slowly pumped enough oxygen in the atmosphere to make our planet habitable for higher forms of life.

A distant seagull gave a long mournful call and I was almost overcome with the ineffable beauty of our planet on this the cusp between winter and spring. But much as I wanted spring to be just around the corner I also knew that the most damaging storms historically occurred in March and April when the beaches and dunes were most vulnerable from having already been torn apart by winter storms.

There was one more thing I wanted to see before sunset. There is a large granite boulder that stands about 5 feet high and is almost 5 feet in diameter sitting on the shore. We have always called it "GiGi's rock" because our dog loved to race down the path and leap up onto the rock in a single bound, especially when there were onlookers to clap in amazement.

But my daughter had returned from walking down the path a few days ago and reported that the rock had moved. Of course this was absurd the rock weighed several tons, but I thought I would check it out anyway. Sure enough the rock had moved about 15 feet up the shore. How could this have happened?

I could see a faint scar where the boulder had scrapped over the gravelly shore, but the biggest clue was a three-inch band of clean granite on the bottom of the boulder. This is where the base of the boulder used to sit in the sediments. Apparently the boulder had become frozen in the ice, which had lifted it up just high enough so it could bump and scrape over the bottom on the incoming tides.

It was an amazing testament to the power of ice in changing the face of the landscape. It was not hard to imagine nature doing the same thing with the boulders in the South Jetty.

I returned home to light a fire and cook up a steaming bowl of chowder for my son and his new girlfriend who were on the way to film in Chile and Peru. Oh to be Fifty again!

CHAPTER 36
"The Sturgeon"
February 16, 2018

This is the type of dredge the state could purchase.

On February 16, the Merrimack River Beach Alliance conducted its regular monthly meeting. It was pretty much "the same old, same old," but with an ominous twist. The Corps of Engineers admitted there was still no funding to dredge the Piscataqua River, and they were waiting for funds to dredge the Merrimack River, which could be dangerously shallow in the coming summer.

But the Corps wanted Newburyport to conduct an expensive Section 204 study just in case. Plus it looked like George Charos was not going to be able to dredge out his docks because his permits would not come through before the piping plover nesting season commenced on April This meant that building the sacrificial dune to protect the houses on Northern Reservation Terrace was dead until autumn, when it probably wasn't going to be needed anyway.

So all of the projects that communities had been spending money to get permits for were on hold. Just to top it off, the Army Corps of Engineers representative, Ed O'Donnell, wryly pointed out that President Trump's budget had requested no money be appropriated for projects in Massachusetts.

This was the problem with relying on a red tape girdled, pork barrel fed, slow moving federal agency that gets it funding from Congress and its budget requests from a president that doesn't like Massachusetts and probably has "Glouchesterphobia".

But State Representative Lenny Mira offered some hope. He had been looking into having the state, Essex County or several North Shore communities purchase their own dredge.

The model for such an acquisition was Barnstable County, which unlike most counties in Massachusetts has a strong presence and brands itself as "the regional government of Cape Cod".

After Cape Cod's Chatham inlet burst open in 1987 the town requested that the Army Corps of Engineers dredge the channel, which was the lifeblood of the third most lucrative fishing port in Massachusetts.

But the process dragged on several agonizingly long years and was only settled in 1992 when President Bush signed the bill when his helicopter landed on the White House lawn, after returning from his loss to Bill Clinton.

Cape Cod's wily Congressman Gerry Studds had attached the Chatham project to the bill, which outlined a trade agreement with the first breakaway republic of the Soviet Union, which he knew the president desperately wanted to sign.

The same problem was true for numerous other towns on Cape Cod. They had expended their own money to get permits for dredging their harbors and renourishing their beaches. The projects had all been permitted but they took years to get funding from the Corps so the projects had languished for decades if they ever got done at all.

Finally Cape Cod had had enough and conducted a cost benefit analysis that found that indeed it did make sense for the county to buy their own dredge. It would be cheaper for both the state, which had previously funded 75% of the projects and the towns, which had to put up 25% to get them done.

Consequently, the state gave the county a million dollar grant to purchase their own dredge, which was christened the *Cod Fish*. Over the past 21 years the *Cod Fish* has removed almost two million cubic yards of sand from 288 projects and 95% of that material went into nourishing Cape Cod's beaches. That stands up well to the amount of sand than the Corps has dredged in the entire New England region during the last twenty years.

Imagine what such a dredge could do for Plum Island. Residents of Northern Reservation Terrace only wanted a measly 2,600 cubic yards of sand and Newbury only wanted ten times that amount.

Lenny explained that now six towns and the state of Maine had hired the Woods Hole group to conduct a feasibility study into purchasing a similar dredge for southern Maine. The Woods Hole Group was the same company that had done the scientific study of Plum Island's currents.

It would make perfect sense for Massachusetts, Essex County and the North Shore towns to hire the same group to look into the feasibility of the North Shore's purchasing their own dredge. If they do I propose that it be named *The Sturgeon*.

CHAPTER 37
Clean Clams
February 21, 2018

Depuration plant.

On February 21, I visited the Massachusetts Depuration plant on the tip of Plum Island's North Point. It would be easy to miss the plant. It sits in a low gray-shingled building with a large loading dock. Every morning trucks arrive from places like Boston, Quincy and Revere to drop off their many bushels of clams. But the clams come from polluted beds so they have to filter in cold salt water and be bathed in Ultraviolet light before they can be sold.

There is a reason the plant is based on Plum Island. When it was originally built the plant piped water in from the Merrimack River. But as the river became polluted the plant managers realized they were just making the clams dirtier, so they drilled two 130-foot deep wells down through the dunes to reach the salt water aquifer. This worked for decades, but ever since the Corps of Engineers repaired the South Jetty, the ocean has been advancing toward the easternmost wellhead.

In September, the ocean was still sixty feet from the wellhead, and protected behind twenty-foot high dunes. But we had watched the ocean steadily claw away the dunes, so that by the end of February the wellhead was less than 9 feet from edge of the dunes and they were only four feet high.

If the river water got into the wellhead it could pollute the entire aquifer. So the plant managers wanted to shut off the wellhead and just use water from the westernmost well, which was about 65 feet further inland.

The plant would have to operate with only half the amount of water but it could limp along this way until new wells were drilled in three to five years. This could still save the livelihoods of about 250 shellfishermen who dug 4.6 million dollars worth of clams from places like Boston, Revere, Lynn and Quincy.

On February 25, workers ran lines from one wellhead to the other trying to find the manhole cover buried in the dunes. Then they could turn off the spigot and isolate the easternmost wellhead before the arrival of an early March storm packing 70 mile an hour winds and 20-foot high waves.

CHAPTER 38
Sandy Point Paella
February 24, 2018

Sandy Point paella.

The sun rose noticeably earlier on February 24. It was still close to the middle of winter and one of our photographers had posted a picture of oysters on Sandy Point.

I figured that nobody would probably be returning shells to such an inaccessible spot, so I decided to load myself up with my waders, clam rake, and a bucket of empty shells I had weathered for just such an occasion.

It is important to return empty shells to the oyster beds because the calcium carbonate coming off the old shells triggers larval oysters to settle on such favorable spots. But I also wanted to see how many oysters had settled on the tip of Sandy Point.

It had started to get a little cloudy by the time I reached the point but it was warm and I decided to push on. The dune grass was already sprouting up through the layers of powdery white sand that had blown over the dunes during the winter storms. The new sand would be held together by the dune grass roots and make the incipient dunes grow almost 6 inches higher.

But it was the lagoon itself that had changed most dramatically. The last time I was out here in November the outflowing water was still undermining the dunes. Now that inlet had closed and there was almost a hundred feet of beach in front of the dune so the tip of Sandy Point had grown 100 feet in just four months.

Water was still flowing over the spit that wrapped around the lagoon, but it was just depositing more sand then exiting out a new smaller inlet on the other side of the 200-foot long body of water.

But one of the most extreme low tides of the year was fast approaching so I shouldered my heavy gear and trudged about a mile up the beach to the end of the point. There, large stone pilings were all that remained of the dock where the steam ferries Carlotta and The General Bartlett would land and disgorge passengers who wended their way to the rustic hotel that overlooked Plum Island Sound.

The building had only been demolished in 2016. When the Fish and Wildlife Service took over the island in 1942 they stipulated that any house could stay in the family until the present owner died. Most of the families kept their houses in the names of the oldest generation but the owners of what had become the Bluff House made the wise decision to put the house in name of their young daughter who lived until she was 88, thus granting four more generations of happy years of camp living.

SANDY POINT PAELLA

Soon I started to see oysters but most of them were the so-called European oysters and most of them were dead. I counted 20 such dead oysters along a 30 foot transect and found only one large living one. The smaller ones had probably succumbed to last winter's cold and ice.

But there were a few bunches of native oysters and many immature ones attached to the rocks. There were also large beds of large juicy blue mussels and even a surf clam. One of the storms had probably dislodged it from a nearby sand island and swept it onto the rocks where it was able to survive even though it could not dig into the substrate.

It was getting late and my gear was getting heavy. The Refuge had made a path out to Ipswich Bluffs after they had demolished the house. I figured the footing would be better if I returned on the path. Big mistake. The path didn't go back to the parking lot where I had left my car but to another lot a mile away, so in the end I had to make a three-mile circuit with my heavy equipment. But at least I had brought along a bag so I didn't have to walk three miles in chest high waders.

But the day was well worth it. My family dined that night on fresh raw oysters, white wine and a Sandy Point Paella garnished with oysters, mussels and chunks of surf clams marinated in olive oil and garlic.

CHAPTER 39
The First March Storm
March 2, 2018

Photographing sand flowing trough the jetty after the March storms.

On March 2, winter storm Riley battered the East Coast with rain, hurricane force gusts and 20-foot high waves. Most damaging of all it lasted through four tidal cycles when the full moon was 30,000 miles closer to the earth than usual, when the earth was closest to the sun and when all these celestial objects were in line.

These factors all translated into enough force to erode the entire front face of Plum Island by ten to twenty feet. But the storm also provided residents and officials with a map to show how to slow erosion in the future.

First, let's look at the southern end of the island. Bar Head is one of the five major glacial drumlins that underlie the island. It is basically a big pile of gravel, rocks and sand deposited by the glaciers at the end of the last Ice Age.

The storm eroded Bar Head back about twenty feet, Vegetation cascaded down the face of the bank and ended up on the boulder field below, then the sand flowed south causing Sandy Point to grow about 50 feet. But nobody ever heard about this because there were no houses on Sandy Point. It was simply a natural phenomenon, nature's way of healing a barrier beach after a storm.

The north end of the island would also like to grow about a 100 feet longer each year. But it is prevented from doing so by the South Jetty.

The damage at this end of the island was totally unnecessary. If the city or state had rebuilt or even just maintained the sacrificial dune the damage could have been greatly reduced or even prevented.

But the most significant feature of this storm was that the center of the island was breached and rebreached during four high tides. Water cascaded down Plum Island Turnpike running into water flowing in from the marsh side of the island. This left the shops, markets and restaurants standing in over a foot of water and the Newbury police closed the island for cars driving on or off the island for four hours every day during the high tides.

This is now the new normal. Whenever the combined height of the waves and high tide is over 20 feet, the island will breach again.

The reason that the breaches occurred was because this spot is immediately north of Center Groin. The same thing happened with the 4 other groins in the groinfield. Waves washed over the seawalls tearing away stairs, garage doors and washing large rocks and seawater into the streets and houses below.
The seawalls had slumped as the waves washed through them. The reason that the new homes had no structural damage is that they were up on pilings, so the waves only washed away garage doors and stairs, rather than slamming into the houses' first floors. But several houses

filled with seawater as the ocean overcame Newbury's drainage systems.

Damage will continue to be inevitable in the center of the island as long as the groins remain. They should have been removed after the 2013 March storm, but at the time people were convinced that this hotspot of erosion was caused by the offshore sandbar growing south. A few people still believe this despite the study done by the Woods Hole Group in 2016.

This sets up an interesting experiment. The state could remove the boulders from Center Groin and observe what happens. The breaching would stop and the beach would grow to be 60 feet wider at high tide and a hundred feet wider at low tides as it is on either sides of the groinfield. Once people saw the changes they could move on to remove the other groins until the center returned to having a broad swimmable beach better able to dissipate energy and slow erosion. Now we would have to wait and see if it would happen.

CHAPTER 40
The Fillet of Sand
March 6, 2018

The Fillet of Sand.

One of my pet peeves is watching reporters stand on a beach waiting for someone's house to topple into the ocean. Nobody ever comes out at low tide the next day to see what really happened.

Consequently, on March 6, I drove to Plum Island to see how much sand the storm had washed through the jetty. A few flakes of snow were whirling out of a pewter sky and the waves were still high even though the tide was dead low.

Every time I come to the beach I discover something new. This time was no exception. As I topped a rise the beach spread out before me. But the dunes in front of the homes on Northern Reservation Terrace were gone, replaced by a broad sloping beach that waves could now ride up and over to flood people's homes. A giant coil of metal cable lay to my right. The storm had unearthed it from below the old Coast Guard station.

But the big surprise was the spur of the jetty. It was almost entirely buried. I could see where waves had swept around the tip of the spur pushing sand over the boulders nearest the dunes. At least five feet of sand had washed up against the spur. For the last four years you had to clamber over five feet of treacherous boulders, now you had a nice sandy path.

Beyond that was an even bigger surprise; a broad new beach hugged the riverside of the jetty. I had seen this before but the beach had never been as long or as broad as it was after this past storm. I had figured I would have to try to pace along the top of the jetty to estimate the length of the new beach, now I could just use this nice sandy path to walk over the jetty and onto the new beach.

And what a beach it was! It was composed of nice white fine-grained sand that had been filtered through the jetty leaving the coarser grained sands behind. First I paced off the width of the beach from the jetty to the river. It was 87 feet wide. Then I started pacing off the length of the new beach but was interrupted by a Coast Guard cutter that swung in close to put four sets of binoculars on me. I guess they wanted to see what a person could possibly be doing walking below the jetty on a freezing day at 8:30 in the morning. I wondered the same thing, but gave them a cheery thumbs up and continued my transect.

The beach was 87 feet wide and 572 feet long, almost the size of two football fields. But they were football fields filled with four to six feet of sand. That meant that up to 96,051 cubic yards of sand had flowed through the jetty during the last four tidal cycles.

But the real significance of this situation was that in just three weeks that sand would snake around the spur and be sitting in front of the houses on Northern Reservation Terrace. You could skim 6,000 to 10,000 cubic yards off the top of the sand and use it to rebuild the sacrificial dune that had worked so well the year before.

If the city and state didn't have the money the residents were willing to pay for a Bob Cat operator themselves. It seemed like this could be expedited since Governor Baker had declared a state of emergency. All that residents had to do was see if they could get permission to go ahead.

One of the residents in Newbury had been given emergency permission to scrape together a 40-foot high dune the night before Hurricane Sandy. Would the residents of Northern Reservation Terrace be given the same permission? We would find out at an emergency meeting of the MRBA hastily scheduled for March 9.

CHAPTER 41
Emergency!
March 9, 2018

Emergency!

Governor Charley Baker declared a state of emergency after "The Power Outage Storm" that left over 300,000 residents of Massachusetts without electricity. The Merrimack River Beach Alliance held its own emergency meeting on March 9. Everyone in Pita Hall was frazzled from lack of sleep, exhaustion and hearing waves rushing under their homes and smashing down walls.

The meeting started with a town-by-town assessment of damages. Newburyport concentrated on the waves that could now ride over the beach and under the houses on Northern Reservation Terrace.

Newbury was in a more precarious situation. All of the 35 houses that had either washed away or been declared uninhabitable a March storm in 2013 had sustained significant damage again.

These included three houses that had been built on exactly the same footprint as the houses that had washed away. Their value had just been battered by the storm and it would probably take five years without storms for prices to rise again to their pre-storm value.

Waves had bludgeoned down walls, torn garage doors off their hinges and swept away stairways from almost every home on the ocean. More importantly, the houses had been undermined by the waves and now were in danger of toppling into the ocean.

But the town had it own a ticklish problem. It had repeatedly made the argument that seawalls were the answer to erosion and clearly they weren't.

The problem with seawalls is that they don't work. The Newbury seawall had failed along its entire half-mile length; waves had scoured sand from behind the seawall so it had collapsed leaving an open gash in the dunes where waves had undermined the homes. Several of them were now leaning over these empty chasms and could topple into the surf at any moment.

The other problem with this seawall was that it was uneven. Several residents had dumped extra boulders on the beach so the seawall bulged out causing end scour. One of these bulges had made the waves wash through the dunes and down the slope where it had overwhelmed Newbury's underground drainage system. This caused several neighbors' basements to fill with water and left a three-foot deep pond in the road. A week after the first storm it was still making the street impassable.

It was cathartic for everyone to tell their stories in the meeting but frustrating that so little time was left to discuss solutions; like roping off the beach so gawkers wouldn't trample down dune grass and rebuilding the sacrificial dunes. But this was the solution that everyone finally focused on.

The Charos family was waiting for permission from the Department of Environmental Protection to dredge under their dock. But the DEP was the 800-pound gorilla NOT in the room. They had stopped attending the meetings after Newbury residents had flaunted the state's regulations. As we spoke the residents were dumping more boulders on their illegal seawall. It might have been understandable if the DEP had written off the entire island.

But they hadn't. They had allowed the Department of Conservation and Recreation who owned North Beach to build the sacrificial dunes the year before. Now the homeowners on Northern Reservation Terrace were willing to raise money so the DCR could rebuild them again.

It was a model project that used proven techniques to build a natural dune. One that the state should encourage and would.

CHAPTER 42
The Silkie
March 11, 2018

My friend waves good bye.

March 11 was a warm sunny day and I had more than a whiff of spring fever. A meeting I was supposed to attend had been cancelled so I decided to take some photos of the center of the island.

As I walked back I noticed a cluster of people crowded around Center Groin. They were watching a beautiful young Harp Seal pup soaking up the sun.

She had swum all the way down from the Arctic Circle in search of herring that were disappearing in the North because of global warming. But now she was resting on the beach after battling the last storm.

She looked at me with beautiful liquid eyes that seemed to suggest humor and curiosity. So I crouched down to look as much like a seal as my creaky old legs would allow and advanced down the groin, sitting first on one boulder then another. She would look back over her shoulder as if she liked my company then would turn and go back to sleep.

If there hadn't been so many people around, I would have lain on the beach and fallen asleep myself. All the time I kept telling her how beautiful she was and thanked her for coming out of the ocean to see me. She answered me with a string of melodious chirps and twitters that give Harp Seals their name. We continued this interspecies duet for most of the afternoon.

After awhile a seal rehabilitator came along and let me get a little closer to take a few more photographs. My friend just sang her song and looked on with friendliness and warmth. But it was finally time to go so I doffed my hat and told her "Have a good night," and turned to go.

But then I heard laughter rippling through the small group of people who had been watching our antics and turned to see my friend waving her flipper at me. So I did the polite thing and waved back trying to mimic her melodious song.

I went home that night, hoping I had given her as much as she had given me. Farewell good friend, may you always stay as happy and healthy as you were on that beach — and for gosh sakes stay away from polar bears!

CHAPTER 43
The Sandy Point Lagoon
March 19, 2018

The Sandy point Lagoon.

March 19 presented a tiny window of opportunity between the third and fourth March storms. The temperatures were still in the Twenties, but the sun was warm and the sky was cobalt blue.

I decided to spend this gift investigating what the storms had done to Sandy Point, but first I had to drive through puddles that were hubcap deep. The day before they had been the size of swimming pools.

The beach was unrecognizable. North of Bar Head drumlin the beach was entirely gone and large rocks and cobble were eroding out of the drumlin that anchored the island in place. But now that condition could become a liability because the island couldn't move landward against the onslaught of storms and sea level rise.

The beach itself was covered with a debris field of logs, plastic boat parts, and intact buoys jutting out of a waist deep bank of vegetation. Enmeshed within the vegetation were dead horseshoe crabs. I had been monitoring the recovery of a small population of the crabs that spawned on the back of the island. Had they also been done in by the storms?

What I really wanted to know was how the lagoon at the tip of Sandy Point had fared, so I slogged through the squishy debris to make sure to arrive before high tide.

It was a considerable shock. The lagoon, which had been long and narrow, was now round and barely a fifth the size it had been the month before. Its old inlet that used to flow so fast it had eroded the sides of the landward dunes had been replaced by an inlet that exited directly into the sound and was now only half an inch deep. It braided through a broad delta of sand that had been deposited by the storms.

It looked like the inlet would continue to drain the lagoon until only a broad field of sand remained. The beautiful lagoon would be gone but it would be replaced. Another spit was curving to the West to encircle a new lagoon. In this manner the beach had grown two hundred feet in less than a month.

Next summer bathers and swimmers would enjoy this nice new broad beach, and fish in the shallow flats that make this end of Sandy Point look like the Bahamian Banks.

Walking back I noticed a broad bank of peat from a marsh that had flourished in this area thousands of years before when Plum Island was still migrating toward the waiting drumlins. It also accounted for the fossilized shells of oysters that appeared on Crane's Beach after such storms. This whole area that had been a large productive marsh was now a beautiful area of beaches and flats for sun bathing and fishing.

But there was a fly in the ointment. As I looked to the North of Bar Head the entire beach was just gone. Swept away by waves that had burst through the dunes, washed through a boardwalk and over the road, threatening to flood Stage Island Pond.

So this was now a permanent new washover area threatening to make Sandy Point into a new island. Such are the ways of erosion and accretion in our world of rapidly rising seas.

CHAPTER 44
Overwash and Breaches
March 23, 2018

Potential breaches, Lot #6.

The March storms left Plum Island with four areas that could be breached by future storms. The most obvious one was at Center Groin. People had watched as waves burst through the dunes and flooded down into the extension of the Plum Island Turnpike. There it had joined with the water flooding in from the marsh to inundate the only road on or off the island.

After each high tide town trucks would plow the sand back up into the parking lot and make a four-foot high berm that would be breached during the next tidal cycle. This had happened during all four March storms.

Such breaching would continue to happen as long as the groin created this sluiceway and whenever the combined height of the tide and waves totaled 21 feet, an expected occurrence during regular winter erosion seasons. But because there was no head of water pressure behind the island the washover area would heal itself as Newbury pushed the sand back into a berm.

The second washover area was on the far end of North Point, where the storms had reduced forty-foot high dunes into seven-foot high midgets in less than a month. In one area the dune was only 3 feet above the beach.

This is where waves had roared through the dunes leaving the wellhead for the State's depuration plant nine feet out in the Merrimack River where it could be contaminated by the river's polluted waters. The break had closed down half the plant's water supply. If the second well was flooded, the livelihoods of hundreds of shellfishermen could be in jeopardy.

Storms would continue to course through this low spot whenever the combined height of the waves and tides exceeded 14 feet, an almost everyday occurrence. The washover would not create a new inlet, but the ocean would continue to incur into the dunes every time there was a storm.

The third washover area was between two houses on Annapolis Way. One of the owners had extended his seawall so it created endscour that had carved out a sluiceway where waves had washed through the dunes and down a hill where they had overwhelmed Newbury's drainage system. This left a three-foot deep pond in the lower road when several people's homes had filled with water.

The area would also not create a permanent inlet but would continue to cause extreme flooding. Boulders placed in the sluiceway would only accelerate water rushing through the dunes and down into the lower road.

But the most severe problem was on the south end of the island, where waves had burst through the dunes in five places. They had destroyed one of the Parker River Wildlife Refuge's most beloved boardwalks and sent ocean water precariously close to Stage Island Pond. This would continue to happen whenever tides totalled more than 19 feet.

The waves had also removed the front 30 to 50 feet of the beach and washed the sand into the swale behind the dunes. This was how the beach rolls over itself to migrate. The entire southern end of the island had moved about 30 feet inland, creating new dunes, beaches and nesting areas for endangered shorebirds.

But the real problem was the height of water in Stage Island Pond. If it was higher than the ocean during the outgoing tide, the tide could scour a new inlet on a single tidal cycle. I had seen an inlet go from being less than an inch to over six feet deep in a week, and 20 feet deep a month later.

The other thing that was happening was that the sand eroding off of Plum Island was filling in the mouth of the Parker River. This would force the river to find a new path of least resistance to flow to the ocean and that could be through the new Stage Pond Inlet.

The Merrimack River had done the same thing in less than three years when it jumped from exiting through what we now call the Basin to its present location half a mile to the north.

The new Stage Island Inlet would make Sandy Point into an island, eventually connected to Ipswich by walkable sandflats. Ipswich would gain over a hundred acres of new beaches, dunes, clamflats and uplands.

Plus, it would only take ten minutes for me to walk from my house in Ipswich to Sandy Point, saving me an hour-long drive to get to the southern end of the island. As my neighbor who also works on Sandy Point sardonically noted, "Huzzah for sea level rise!"

CHAPTER 45
Two Steps Ahead, Three Steps Back
April 4, 2018

Two steps forward, three steps back.

On April 4, the Newburyport Department of Public Services started building the sacrificial berm to protect the houses on Northern Reservation Terrace. It was a bit of a Rube Goldberg affair.

First someone had to excavate upland sand out of a quarry in Maine, then transport it to Plum Island where the DPS workers used skid and turn excavators to finally layer the foreign sand onto the dunes.

Meanwhile you had 97,000 cubic yards of compatible sand that had just filled in the cove behind the spur of the jetty. All the city or residents had to do would be to get permission to pay a Bob Cat operator to push the top layer of sand up the beach and shape it into a berm.

But the state had already permitted using the more expensive upland sand, so at least the project was underway. It also had broad public support. Fifty people had shown up the week before to clear last summer's fencing off the site, forty additional people had shown up to clean up Sandy Point and more would return to help plant the dunegrass behind the berm.

Hannah Gross had convinced sixteen of her friends, classmates and several community leaders to clean up Plum Island Point. It was part of her Bat Mitzvah service project held in the memory of Reizel Gross who had died in the Holocaust. The public understood that this was the right way to work with nature, and each other, to protect a beloved barrier beach.

But instead of inviting the press to cover this positive story, residents had convinced Boston's Channel Five television station to do a lengthy piece about building seawalls on Plum Island in 2013. It was like rubbing salt in old wounds.

The piece starred Bob Connors who had never met a television camera he didn't like. He coyly thanked former governor Duval Patrick for letting Newbury residents build their illegal seawalls.

But Bob failed to mention that he sat on the board of the Pacific Legal Foundation, the most powerful anti-environmental organization in the United States, and he had convinced their lawyers to threaten to sue the state if he didn't get his way. The state backed down in half and hour but the bad blood had remained.

The head of the Department of Environmental Protection had resigned to have his back fixed from the strain of attending meetings on the island, and DEP employees stopped coming to the Merrimack River Beach Users Alliance meetings.

DEP was still in no mood to grant favors to Plum Island and it threatened to shut down the berm project when the city's plover monitor quit on the second day.

It was all a bit disheartening. Several groups had spent the last five years inviting some of the top coastal engineers in the country to give talks on how to protect barrier beaches. The Merrimack Valley Regional Planning Authority had hired a group of geologists from Woods Hole to conduct a study that the Army Corps of Engineers should have done before repairing the south jetty – the jetty that had stopped the natural flow of sand to Northern Reservation Terrace.

For every two steps forward there seemed to have been three steps backwards. As soon as a storm hit the same old voices succumbed to the same old siren song of using seawalls and boulders to fight the Atlantic Ocean. Their seawalls had failed and been rebuilt so many times they were almost more expensive than some of the houses they were supposed to protect.

I was so disheartened by the situation that I decided to not jump into the fray. But then something totally unexpected happened. People started writing about the situation in the papers and on local Internet sites.

They had been listening after all. They knew that barrier beaches need to be able to move, pulsate, and grow. They knew that seawalls didn't work for their owners and made matters worse for their neighbors. They understood that repairing the Merrimack River's south jetty had put houses at risk on Northern Reservation Terrace and they applauded the people who had cleaned up the beaches and funded the construction of the sacrificial berm.

Nobody wanted to return to the days of hiring high priced lawyers and lobbyists to flaunt environmental regulations and the basic tenants of coastal geology.

It seemed like a good time to move on to writing about nearby Crane's Beach that had no erosion problem, because it had no houses to wash into the ocean.

Two Steps Ahead, Three Steps Back